An a... gly less subst... he ...ance is per... ...ut even a minute amounts can affect an allergy prone individual. These substances include pollen, spores of fungi, house dust, eggs, fish, wheat, nickel, ...mium, penicillin etc., — all harmless except to ...e who are allergic.

...ne of the commonly seen ailments among ...rgic patients are asthma, rashes, diarrhoea, ...ominal cramps, anaphylactic reaction, contact ...matitis etc. However these and other allergy ...blems can be prevented and successfully ...anaged. Based on results of latest research and ...dvances in medical science, and the author's own ...perience, this book is a source in invaluable ...formation to all who may have allergy problems in ...e family or amongst friends.

... comprehensive and readily understandable book... the ...thor not only explains the nature of allergy problems ...t tells how a patient can learn what is causing the ...action ... (this book is) a must for doctors and general ...actitioners and patients of chronic asthma.

The Hindu

The Author

Prof. Dr O.P. Jaggi is a medical scientist of international standing. He is the former Dean of the faculty of Medical Sciences, University of Delhi, and Director of V. Patel Chest Institute, Delhi.

He firmly believes in the concept of preventive medicine and, therefore, in explaining medical facts. He has written and spoken extensively on health and medicine, both in India and abroad. His books on healthcare including *Cancer: Causes, Prevention & Treatment; Asthma in Children; Healing Systems* and *You Can Prevent Heart Attack* have been immensely popular. His deep commitment to patient care has won him wide recognition.

He can be contacted at Asthma, Chest and Allergy Centre, 128, Vasant Enclave, New Delhi-110 057.

Asthma and Allergies

Causes, Prevention and Treatment

Dr O P Jaggi

Orient
Paperbacks
DELHI | MUMBAI | HYDERABAD

www.orientpaperbacks.com

ISBN 13: 978-81-222-0039-3
ISBN 10: 81-222-0039-7

1st Published 1985
2nd Revised Edition 1988
14th Printing 2009

Asthma and Allergies: Causes, Prevention & Treatment

© Dr. O.P. Jaggi, 1985

Cover design by Vision Studio

Published by
Orient Paperbacks
(A division of Vision Books Pvt. Ltd.)
5A/8, Ansari Road, New Delhi-110 002

Printed in India at
Saurabh Printers Pvt. Ltd., Noida

Cover Printed at
Ravindra Printing Press, Delhi-110 006

Contents

Preface

Asthma and allergies are more manageable than most other diseases. They can be prevented from occurring, and they can be controlled if they have already occurred. This, however, can be achieved only if the patients know the fundamental facts about them. Essentially, this book describes ways and means:

1. to recognize that a particular set of symptoms is allergic in nature;
2. to find out what is the cause of these allergic symptoms; and
3. to take measures to get rid of the allergic condition.

My experience with the patients—including near and dear ones—of asthma and other allergies, indicates that the best method of helping them is to educate them to look after themselves.

There are numerous examples of asthma patients who have managed themselves so well as not only to overcome it, but also, some of them, to gain international reputation in athletic events and sports. This they have been able to do because of proper understanding of the condition and their own guts to challenge it. If they can, why not you?

V. Patel Chest Institute   O.P. JAGGI
University of Delhi.

1

Introduction

Allergy is a reaction of the body to a harmless substance. Substances like pollens of the flowers, spores of the fungi, house dust, eggs, fish, wheat, or nickel, chromium, and penicillin, are harmless to all people, except those who are allergic to them. Pollens, fungal spores and house dust can cause recurrent bouts of sneezing or asthma; foods like eggs, fish, wheat can cause rashes, cramps in the abdomen, diarrhoea; nickel and chromium can cause reaction in the skin (contact dermatitis), and penicillin can cause anaphylactic reaction, in which there is sudden collapse of the person allergic to it.

The substance that causes reaction in an allergic person is called *allergen* or *antigen*. The substance produced in the body of an allergic person as a result of the introduction of an allergen or antigen, is called *antibody*. When antigen and antibody meet together and react, the process is called *antigen-antibody reaction*.

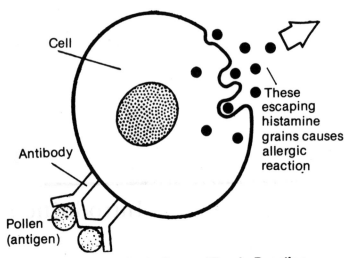

Cell

These escaping histamine grains causes allergic reaction

Antibody

Pollen (antigen)

How Pollen Grain Cause Allergic Reaction

Antigen-antibody reactions are of various types depending upon the nature of both the antigen and the antibody as well as other factors; one of which is the mode of introduction of the antigen.

An asthma-prone person has in his blood and organs, the antibody, which is called *reagin*; it is a type of gamma globulin, in short form called IgE.

IgE in the blood or organ, resides on the surface of a cell called *mast cell.* When an antigen reacts with IgE present on the surface of the mast cell, among other things, there occurs the rupture of the mast cell wall, and from it substances like histamine, slow-reacting substance of anaphylaxis, serotonin and many others, are released during allergic reactions. These are the substances which cause the manifestations of allergy, like spasm of the muscles of the lung airways in asthma, or exudation of fluid from the nasal mucous membrane in cases of seasonal sneezing, or irritation, swelling and redness of the skin in cases of urticaria etc.

14

Asthma, seasonal or perennial sneezing, urticaria and eczema are many and different manifestations of one condition—allergy. A person may have eczema in childhood, develop sneezing when he grows up and then may have instead of these manifestations, or over and above them, asthma. A parent may have asthma and his one son may have eczema and another a tendency to get sneezing. What is inherited is allergy, and not a particular manifestation of allergy.

The best way to get rid of allergic reactions is to find out to what one is allergic and then to avoid any contact with it.

However, this is not easy. The first problem is that, many a time, it is difficult to be sure as to what one is allergic to. Secondly, some allergic substances—and this is more important in cases of asthma—that are present in the air that we breathe in, cannot be avoided.

2

What is Asthma?

Bronchial asthma, commonly called asthma, consists of repeated attacks of breathlessness and wheezing. When the patient is not in an attack, he feels normal. When an asthma patient comes in contact with an allergic substance, it behaves, as an antigen and reacts with the corresponding antibodies already present in his body. The histamine and other substances liberated during the allergic reactions cause the following changes in the bronchi:

1. Bronchial muscles are constricted to the extent of lessening the diameter (calibre) of the bronchi.
2. Mucous membrane of the bronchi gets swollen, which further restricts the lumen of the bronchi.
3. Secretions are poured out from the swollen mucous lining into the constricted lumen of the bronchi.

When the bronchi are constricted and they are full of secretions, the patient has difficulty in breathing

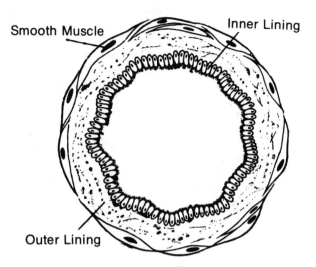

Normal Bronchus

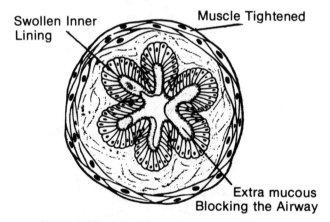

Constricted Bronchus During an Attack

A Cross-Section of a Normal and Constricted Bronchial Tube

and his breath has a wheezing sound in it, which is more on breathing out because then the bronchi get narrower.

Asthma is a disease of the larger and medium-sized airways of the lungs and there is obstruction to outflow of air from the lungs. Since enough air does not reach the lungs for the exchange of gases, there is hurried breathing to compensate it.

Cough is a frequent symptom in asthmatics. This occurs in order to throw out the excessive secretions produced in the lungs. This is particularly so in those who have respiratory infection as well. Cough gets relieved by the same measures as breathlessness.

The airways of the asthmatics are over-reactive to pollens, air pollution, changes in temperature, physical

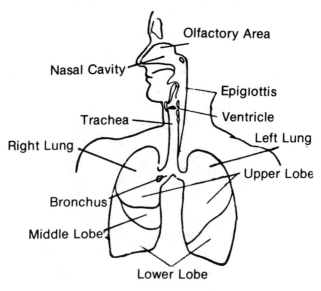

Respiratory Tract

18

excercise, etc., and they react strongly to these factors. Persons who are asthmatics find it extremely difficult to tolerate smoking or air-pollution. Smoke or strong fumes, smell of fresh paint, white-washing, house-dust, or dust from old files, or the opening of dusty almirahs or trunks cause symptoms in some patients.

.Asthma patients are liable to some complications such as thoracic deformity in children, diminished growth, recurrent infection or pneumonia, chronic bronchitis and hyper-inflation of the lung tissues (emphysema).

Types of Asthma

Bronchial asthma can be categorized, depending upon the predominant factors that cause the disease. This categorization is helpful in the treatment of the individual case.

Extrinsic Asthma: The patients have an inherited liability to develop asthma when exposed to allergic agents like pollens, house dust, certain fungi, etc. These patients have, many a time, other manifestations

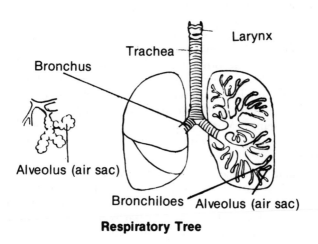

Respiratory Tree

19

of allergy as well, such as recurrent bouts of sneezing (rhinitis) and eczema. These patients benefit from anti-allergy treatments of different types. This type of asthma occurs in the early period of life.

Intrinsic Asthma: These patients do not seem to have an allergic background, but develop the disease because of some pre-existing disease of the lung such as past infections or existing diseases like chronic bronchitis. These patients do not respond well to anti-allergic measures. This type of asthma occurs in the later period of life.

There is another type of asthma which occurs in some people after taking exercise. This is called *exercise induced asthma*. This occurs more commonly when physical exercise is done in cold weather.

What is not Asthma?

Chronic Bronchitis: In an elderly patient, the main difficulty arises in distinguishing asthma from chronic bronchitis and emphysema; sometimes asthma and chronic bronchitis may coexist in a patient. A patient may begin with asthma because of an allergy to pollens, etc., and if improperly or inadequately treated he may develop chronic bronchitis and later on emphysema, as well. On the other hand, a patient may begin with chronic bronchitis, and after many years, develop so-called intrinsic asthma, without any apparent allergic background or known cause and end up as a case of emphysema. Many a time, it is difficult to establish which is the primary disease, and which the complicated one.

Cardiac Asthma: An important disease which simulates bronchial asthma is cardiac asthma. In this condition the breathlessness is, primarily, due to heart disease. This condition also occurs in paroxysms of breathlessness, usually in sleep, but at times also due to exertion. An attack, usually rises to a peak, is accompanied by difficulty in breathing both during inspiration and expiration, and frequently by a terrifying sense of suffocation which causes the patient to sit up or stand erect and even to go to the window for air. The attacks last from a few minutes to a few hours, averaging about an hour, and leave the patient in an exhausted condition for hours or even days.

Cardiac asthma is precipitated by acute failure of the pumping action of the left ventricle of the heart. It is a common feature with hypertensive heart disease and coronary artery disease.

During an attack, the presence of cardiac asthma should be suspected if the patient is more than forty years old; if he has a previous history of hypertension or heart disease; if he is sweating profusely; if he seeks for fresh air; and if he has a sudden fear of death.

Hysterical Asthma: Some patients, in particular young girls, claim the complaint of asthma but history and examination reveal that all they have is sighing respiration; there is no wheeze and no difficulty in either breathing in or breathing out. Such cases present no serious problem in differential diagnosis.

Other Conditions: Diseases which at some stage may simulate bronchial asthma are malignant tumors of the chest, such as lymphosarcoma and Hodgkin's disease. Pressure of enlarged glands in lung cancer may also give rise to wheezing and breathlessness. The same may happen with the dilatation and swelling (aneurysm) of the wall of the aorta in the chest. Aorta is the most important blood vessel which carries the pure blood from the heart for the rest of the body.

Some of the diseases caused by inhalation of different types of dusts, vegetative and non-vegetative (organic and inorganic) can also give rise to symptoms akin to bronchial asthma. With inorganic dust, the history of the patient or his occupation usually reveals a true diagnosis. In the case of organic dust, it becomes difficult to make a diagnosis unless all laboratory investigations are undertaken.

21

Diagnosis of asthma does sometimes pose a problem in children and in elderly people; in young adults the diagnosis rarely presents difficulty.

Could You Be a Potential Asthmatic?

		Yes	No
1.	History of Asthma in the Family	☐	☐
2.	Do you have coughing at the change of season?	☐	☐
3.	Do you have bouts of sneezing at the change of season?	☐	☐
4.	Do you have a running nose?	☐	☐
5.	Do you often have throat infection?	☐	☐
6.	Do you get breathlessness after exertion of the change of season?	☐	☐
7.	Do you have breathing problem when the wind blows?	☐	☐
8.	Do you work/live in a polluted environment?	☐	☐

The more 'Yes' you have, the more chances you have of having Asthma.

Asthma Due to Plant Pollens

Pollens occur in the powder-like substance seen in some of the flowers. Pollen grains are very small in size. In a majority of cases, they are yellow in colour.

Only some of the pollens cause asthma. Out of thousands of different pollens, only about a hundred are known to cause this disease. A plant must have the following characteristic features before its pollens can be suspected of being the cause.

1. The pollen of this plant must be carried by wind for pollination purposes. (There are other plants which are pollinated by insects, water or by self-pollination).
2. The pollen should be sufficiently light for it to be carried over long distances by the wind.
3. The pollen must be produced in abundance.
4. The pollen must have chemical qualities to act as an allergen.

Plants which pollinate through wind, have flowers

which are usually unattractive in appearance, are comparatively small in size; rarely have any smell and contain no nectar. Their pollens are light, dry and abundant in quantity. They are carried over to long distance, sometimes even for hundreds of miles.

Pollens are released from the flowers very early in the morning, often before sunrise. Hense many patients of asthma, sensitive to pollens, have their symptoms at that time. Different asthma patients are allergic to different pollens; some only to one pollen but most of them to more than one. Pollens of common garden flowers such as roses, marigold, phlox, do not cause asthma; their pollens are too heavy, large and sticky, and do not float about in the air.

Pollen Calendar

In order to establish whether an asthma patient is allergic to pollens, and if so to which pollens, detailed investigations are necessary.

First of all, it is necessary to find out which plants—trees, shrubs, grasses and weeds—are present in the area. This needs surveying, identification and cataloguing of all the plants that grow throughout the year or in any one particular season.

The next step is to ascertain which pollens are present in the air in the area under study in different months of the year. This is done by exposing to the air vaseline-coated glass slides, placed in an instrument called pollen-catcher. The pollen-catcher is placed on top of a building, in different localities, where there is a free flow of air. The pollens present in the air, on passing over the slides, get caught in the vaseline. These slides are then examined under a microscope and the type and number of different pollens are counted. This is done daily, throughout the year, and for three to five years. From these extensive observations, one comes to know: 1) the types of pollen present, 2) the month in which they are present and 3) their respective quantities. Thus, one can chart out a pollen calendar for the area.

24

Knowledge of the pollen calendar of an area is absolutely necessary for investigating a case of asthma. If, for instance, an asthma patient says that he gets symptoms in the month of March and April only, it is necessary that we know which pollens are present in the air during these two months.

Pollens in Delhi*

Delhi atmosphere is never entirely free from pollens. During autumn (mid-September to mid-November), spring (mid-February to mid-April) and early summer (mid-April to mid-May) pollens are in abundance, and the incidence of seasonal asthma is very high. Even perennial asthma patients show an aggravation of their symptoms during these seasons. On the other hand, there are less pollens in the air from June to mid-August, and mid-November to mid-February; these are also the months when hay fever and asthma patients have some relief from their symptoms.

Trees contribute 30 per cent of the pollens in the air; significant among them are salvadora, prosopis, terminalia, ailanthus, ricinus and ehretia. Weeds contribute 38 per cent of the pollens in the Delhi air; the important ones are chenopodium, xanthium, amaranthus, cannabis, artemesia, rumex and umbellifers. Of these xanthium alone contributes 18 per cent. Grasses contribute 20 per cent of the pollens in the air; these are cynoden, cenchrus, sorghum, eragrostis, imperata and heteropogon.

The number of pollens in the atmosphere in an area vary from year to year depending upon meteorological conditions such as rainfall, temperature, sunshine, wind-velocity, wind-direction, etc. If there is excessive rainfall before the pollination season, it

*Since no elaborate and long term research work in this regard has been done in other parts of the country, herein the findings from Delhi alone are stated.

stimulates profuse and vigorous growth of the plants with a consequent increase in pollen production. Heavy rains during the pollen season, on the other hand, may interfere with the shedding of pollen or wash it down from the air.

That is one of the reasons why a patient allergic to pollens, gets different grades of symptoms from year to year.

4

Asthma Due to Fungi

During the rainy season, all of us have noticed that if bread is left unused for a few days, a green fibrous growth appears on it; this happens also if a pair of shoes is left unused for a few days in the same weather. These fibrous growths, which appear in humid weather, are moulds or fungi.

Fungi are simple plants, very small in size. They have no chlorophyll, hence they cannot synthesize their own food. They have a growing, vegetative part, made up of long branches called mycelia. They generally reproduce by means of spores.

Most of the fungi perform a useful function in nature. They act as scavengers, converting live and dead material into basic chemicals, which in turn nurture into new life. Antibiotics like penicillin and streptomycin, have been made from them. Alcohol, wine, cheese and certain bakery products are made by using fungi.

Fungi grow best between 20°C to 32°C, though some of them can grow at colder temperatures, like those inside a refrigerator. They survive freezing for months and lie dormant. Temperatures approaching the boiling point of water, kill most of them. For rapid growth, they need humidity to be above 70 per cent. The warm and humid environment inside rooms, or storage places, even shoes, is ideal for their growth.

In the house, furniture dust and mattress dust are particularly good harbourers of fungi. Fungi also attack paper, paint wood, etc. They have been found on rubber gaskets around refrigerator doors. Damp places, like basements are fertile grounds for their growth.

Home gardens breed fungal spores constantly. They grow abundantly on rotting leaves and foliage. The soils of potted house plants and the plants themselves become infected with fungi. Cut flowers and leaves may be contaminated even before they are brought into the house. Fields and areas where grain is grown, processed or stored also have an immense number of spores of the fungi. In the case of many fungi, cow or buffalo dung is the exclusive source of origin. In

Decaying Vegetation the Abode of Moulds

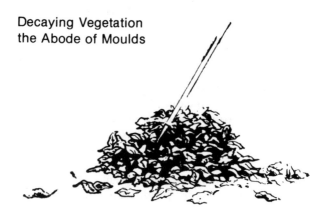

India, cow and buffalo dung are still used as domestic fuel and these form one of the principal source materials of fungi.

Fungi are present in many foods, some are put in intentionally while others enter as contaminants. Mature cheese depends on fungi for its distinctive taste. Yeasts are used in the manufacture of beer and wine and in the preparation of bread and certain cakes. Baked foods often become · mouldy, especially in humid weather, even though they are sterile after taken out of the oven. Potatoes and onions are common sources of contamination when brought into the home.

Because of their light weight and minute size, the spores of the fungi are readily carried about by wind. Spores of the fungi are readily carried in the air for hundreds of miles. They are very resistant to killing.

Not all the viable fungal spores in the air are allergenic. Important allergenic fungi include phoma, mucor, *aspergillus tamarii* and candida.

Next to pollens, spores of different fungi present in the air are the commonest cause of allergy leading to asthma.

In order to treat fungus-sensitive patients, the physician must be familiar with the fungi in the air. He must know the seasons when the common fungi are at their heaviest concentration in the atmosphere of the area. Identification of the fungi and making of their calendar is similar to that of pollens, though it is more tedious.

Delhi, for which a fungal survey has been done, has a high percentage of fungal spores throughout the year. The peak periods of fungal spore concentration are the months of September to November, and February to April, *i.e.*, autumn and spring respectively. In the rainy season the spore concentration is low as the fungal spore, as well as other contaminants of the air, have been settled down by the rain.

The most frequent fungal spores trapped and identified on slides from the Delhi atmosphere are those of alternaria, cladosporium, small round spores, curvularia and heminthosporium; these form 82 per cent of the total fungal flora trapped by exposed slides.

Characteristics of Fungus-Sensitive Patients

Patients having the following symptoms can be suspected of being allergic to fungi:

1. Those having perennial symptoms.
2. Those with perennial symptoms which become severe between September and November, and between February and April.
3. Those allergic to house dust or pollens and who do not do well under specific treatment.
4. Those who show symptoms after ingestion of mould-containing foods and beverages.
5. Those who develop symptoms on exposure to hay, straw, compost,. dead leaves while harvesting, ploughing, harrowing and doing other out-door activities.

Only a small percentage of mould-sensitive patients are sensitive to moulds alone; most of them are allergic to pollens as well.

Among mould-sensitive patients, bronchial asthma is the most frequent predominant symptom. Precautions ought to be taken to make the environments of mould-sensitive patients as free from moulds as possible. Some of these precautions are as follows:

1. Avoid basements.
2. Walls should not absorb moisture; therefore, plastered and painted walls are to be preferred.
3. All rooms and spaces inside the house should have effective ventilation.
4. Potted plants should not be kept in-doors.

5

Asthma Due to House Dust

We have, over the years, seen many cases of asthma having their symptoms only during the Diwali season. Our investigations have shown that it is not the Diwali weather which is detrimental to the health of these people. It is the customary cleaning of the house among north Indians at this time which raises so much dust that those who are allergic to it, experience symptoms of asthma.

What is House Dust?

House dust consists of many things. It has in it the dust that comes from clothes, furnishings, beddings, and pillows; from pets, if there are any; from the parts of the insects in the house; the fungi that grow everywhere; from food remnants; from the human skin and hair; it also contains the outside dust which comes in with the wind. If the furniture, furnishings, beddings, carpets and rugs are old, more house dust is produced from them. If such house dust is not normally visible it can be seen in the shafts of sunlight that enter a room. These motes or particles gradually settle down in the form of house dust.

Mites in House Dust

People allergic to house dust as a who were found not to be allergic to each of the above-mentioned constituents. The true nature of house dust antigen remained a mystery till 1964, when a Dutch research team demonstrated that it was the common house dust mite called *dermatopagoides pteronyssinus* which caused the allergenicity in house dust. Later on, other allergenic mites were also discovered in the house dust. In some samples of house dust over 200 mites in 1 gm of it have been found.

Mite

Mites feed and grow on the constituents of house dust. The common house mite, is relatively small (about one-third of a millimetre in length). It can become airborne during bedmaking, and is present in great numbers in and on mattresses. It grows best, though very slowly, in high humidity (80 per cent), at an optimal temperature of 25°C, and preferably on human dander. It prefers high humidity and moderate temperature.

Improvement in some asthmatic patients on admission to hospital may be the result of reduced exposure to the allergens associated with the house mite. Also aggravation of asthma on going into the bedroom or while in bed may reflect the larger amounts of it in the bedding and the bedroom.

Allergy to house dust is quite common. In a study conducted by me, skin tests were done against different pollens, fungi and dusts on 462 patients of asthma. It was found that 286 (61.9 per cent) were positive to house dust either singly or in combination with other allergens.

Those who are allergic to house dust, must avoid it. The bedroom must be scrupulously clean and uncluttered. All upholstered furniture, rugs, window drapes, and dust-catching ornaments must be removed. The almirah should contain only the patient's current clothing and should be as dust-free as the room itself. Mattresses and pillows should be made of foam rubber. The room should be cleaned with a damp cloth.

6

Asthma Due to Food Articles

llergy to different foods is a well recognized phenomenon. Hippocrates, the famous Greek physician generally regarded as father of medicine in the fifth century B.C., was perhaps, one of the first to record a case of stomach upset and vascular reaction to the skin (urticaria) in a patient who took milk. Another Greek physician and medical writer Galen in the second century A.D., described a case of allergy to goat's milk. Numerous reports of allergy to different foods are available.

The ingestion of foods to which the patient is sensitive may produce a variety of symptoms which include itching and swelling of the lips, sores in the mouth, vomiting, gaseous distension, diarrhoea, urticaria, headache. Symptoms around the mouth may appear immediately, while others appear some time later. The same food at some particular season may produce symptoms, while in others it may not. This depends upon the combination with other allergic factors.

Symptoms of allergy to food taken may appear either soon after, or several hours later; in the latter case, it becomes difficult to identify the offending article, of diet.

Food allergy is more common in infants and children. As the child grows older, he is exposed to many more environmental factors. That is why adults are frequently sensitive not only to foods but also to pollens, dusts, moulds, etc., as well.

Milk Allergy

Cow's milk is not an uncommon allergen in infancy, probably because it is the major foreign protein food during the early months of life. It has been estimated that milk allergy occurs approximately in 0.5 per cent of children.

Milk allergy manifests itself by a variety of symptoms. The commonest symptom is that of the infant feeling unwell when he is put on a milk other than that of his mother, and a need is felt to change from one milk to another. Other symptoms pertain to alimentary tract and the respiratory tract. There may also be eczema or urticaria.

Whenever possible the infant should be breast-fed. This reduces the chances of the development of allergic symptoms. Giving of cow's milk should be delayed up to the age of 9 months to a year in a potentially allergic child.

Many a time, the diagnosis is missed because allergy to milk is not suspected. The best way to make a diagnosis is by eliminating milk from the diet and then rechallenging—the process to administer antigen to evoke an immunological response. Milk must be elimmated from the diet for at least two weeks. If during this period there is marked improvement in the health of the child, or when reintroduction of milk brings back the symptoms, the diagnosis is established.

After the diagnosis is clinched, the offending milk must be removed from the diet. Milk prepared from soya beans is a good substitute. If it is not locally available, it can be prepared in the house.

The soya bean milk should be given upto a year or so and then a re-trial could be made with the offending milk. If the child does not tolerate it, soya bean milk may continue to be given; if few symptoms appear then the cow's milk may gradually be added in the diet.

Soya bean milk is as nutritious as the mother's milk; however, this needs to be supplemented with vitamins and minerals.

Wheat Allergy

Next to milk, wheat is the commonest source of food allergy. This is detected when the infant for the first time is given cereal, and develops a rash, abdominal colic or diarrhoea.

An older child or an adult may have asthma or a patch of eczema which is found to be improved by not taking wheat in any form. The treatment is avoidance of wheat in all its different preparations. Duration of avoidance is decided by trying it and seeing whether it reproduces the symptoms.

Egg Allergy

White of an egg is pure albumin (a protein) and being a foreign protein, it is a potent source of allergy. Taking of a raw egg by a person allergic to it, can cause a most severe reaction, including collapse and shock. Even the smell of egg's contents can cause allergic reactions in highly sensitive people.

Fish Allergy

Fish and other sea foods are amongst the most potent

allergic agents. There is cross reaction between various sea foods. Those who have reaction to fish should avoid other sea foods as well. Here again, even the smell of fish can produce urticaria in some people who are strongly allergic to it.

Most of the nuts, e.g., almond, walnut can cause allergic reactions. Persons who are allergic to them, have to avoid them and also preparations like cakes and cookies containing nuts.

Other foods to which people are commonly allergic are: apples, bananas, cashew nuts, oranges, lemons, grapefruit, mushrooms, watermelons, cucumbers, grapes, *gur* (not cane-sugar), mustard, radish, onions, garlic, chocolates and soft drinks.

Diagnosis

A thorough history of the patient is of the greatest help in diagnosis. Other procedures that help are *elimination diets*. Skin tests in food allergy are not of much help.

Elimination Diets: The patient is instructed to note on a piece of paper all the food he takes and the symptoms, if any, they produce. By studying these daily reports for two to three weeks, one can often detect the onset of symptoms after a new food or after the repeated use of a certain food. The elimination of these foods from the diet one by one, should result in disappearance of symptoms, and the intentional ingestion should be followed by symptoms.

The difficulty arises when the offending food is either milk, egg or wheat, each of which is a common ingredient of many other foods so that its presence is not generally suspected by the patient. It is incumbent on the patient to study and know the ingredients of the food he consumes, so that, he may be better able to avoid any or all of these foods in his diet.

Skin Tests: Many a time, there is no correlation

between the skin tests and the clinical trials with a food. This is because the tests are made with foods extracted in the raw state but eaten in the cooked state, and it has been shown that the cooking of some foods may denature them to the extent that they may be tolerated in limited amounts even by individuals sensitive to them. While food trials are being conducted, it is essential that all other treatment remains unchanged.

The best method of treating food allergies is to find out the incriminating food and to avoid it. While eliminating one food, it is necessary that a non-allergenic substitute of equivalent food value be added to maintain nutrition and avoid monotony. Desensitization to foods is seldom resorted to.

Where the offender cannot be identified, one can only depend on symptomatic therapy. Along with this, the patient is advised to take, as far as possible, cooked foods, which, being denatured, are less allergenic.

7

Asthma Due to Insects

Insect bites normally cause pain and swelling. This is due to the effect of the venom. The degree of reaction produced depends upon the type and quantity of venom introduced. But in some people the venom acts as an antigen and, with the antibodies already present, causes an allergic reaction.

In relation to the allergic reactions produced, the insects may be divided into two groups: the stinging insects and the biting insects.

Biting-Insect Allergy

Allergic reaction to biting insects such as mosquitoes, sandfly etc., is not immediate; it is a delayed one. After several hours of the bite, there appears redness and swelling around the site bitten. There may be some rise in temperature of the body. However, the reaction is never serious, never fatal.

This reaction needs no treatment, except occasionally a tablet of antihistamine to check itching. As the season advances, after many such bites, the body reacts less to them. That is also the reason why these reactions are more severe in children than adults or older people.

Stinging-Insect Allergy

Stinging insects such as bee, wasp and hornet produce an immediate allergic reaction. This may vary from local redness and swelling to the redness of the whole part, or even generalized swelling, urticaria, choking, difficulty in breathing, unconsciousness and death.

Those who have hay fever, eczema, asthma and drug reaction are more liable to get different grades of severe reactions to stinging insects. Establishing diagnosis is easy from the history of the patient.

The best prophylaxis is to avoid situation where one can be stung by the insects and keep the body well covered while going outdoors in the fields and gardens. As soon as a person is stung, he should try to remove the sting from the site with a pin or needle without rubbing it in.

If the sting is on a limb, tie a tourniquet—an appliance for compressing the blood vessels—tightly just above the site of the sting. This would avoid spread of the. venom in the whole body. Loosen the tourniquet a bit every five minutes or so and then remove it after half an hour or so. If possible and available, apply an ice-pack to the area of sting. Take an antihistamine tablet.

Honey Bee   Bumble Bee

If the past experience indicates severe reactions to the stings, it is essential for the person to keep a syringe and an ampoule of adrenaline (1:1000 solution) with him and inject 1/2 to 1 ml of it subcutaneously in the outer side of the thigh, and then report to the nearest doctor or dispensary.

Hyposensitization against the sting venoms of different insects is practised now-a-days with very good results.

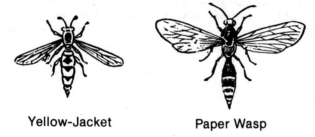

Yellow-Jacket   Paper Wasp

Wasps

Allergy to Insect Remnants

Besides insect bites, another type of hypersensitivity to insects discovered lately is the one related to their remnants. Insects have a very short life span and when they die, their bodies, wings, etc., disintegrate and become part of the dust. During the monsoon, millions of insects appear for a day and die. It has been discovered that some people become allergic to the remnants of the insects and when exposed to such a dust, experience allergic symptoms such as asthma. In many of them, the symptoms appear only in a particular season. Previously such cases were thought to be allergic to a certain pollen appearing in that particular season, but when it was discovered that these gave negative reactions, it was thought that either the relevant pollen had been omitted from the pollen calendar or that they were allergic to something else

41

in the atmosphere in that particular season. Further research revealed that these patients were allergic to the insects present in that season. Some patients are allergic to insects that are perennial and hence they have their symptoms throughout the year.

Just as a calendar is prepared for the pollens and fungi, so also is a calendar made for insects and correlated with the symptoms of the patient in a particular season.

Patients allergic to insects may be allergic to pollens, moulds and dusts as well. Hence, while being treated they have to be hyposensitized against all the offending allergens so as to get maximum benefit.

8

Asthma Due to Animals

Henry Hyde Salter has provided the first accurate description of the attacks of asthma on exposure to a cat. In his book on asthma published around the middle of the nineteenth century, he states:

"This singular phenomena is, I imagine, almost peculiar to myself. The cause of this asthma is the proximity of a common domestic cat; the symptoms are very similar to those of hay fever, and, as in the case of hay fever, are occasioned by some sudden influence inappreciable by the senses. I cannot recollect at what time I first became subject to the cat asthma, but I believe the susceptibility has existed from the earliest period of life. I believe there are even some asthma symptoms even if I were sitting by the fire and the cat sleeping on the hearthrug; but the effect is much greater when the cat is at the distance of about one or two feet, or still closer; it is still further increased by the rising of the fur and moving and rubbing about; but most of fur and moving and rubbing about; but most of all when they are in the lap; just under the face....The asthmatic spasm is immediate and violent, accompanied with sneezing, burning and watery condition of the eyes and nose, and excessive itching of the him....I believe that if the cause were suffered to continue, all or most of the other symptoms of hay fever would ensue, only with a more excessive and conspicuous asthma. After the removal of the cause, and if the paroxysm is not very severe, the cure is effected in five or ten minutes, leaving, as in all other cases of asthmatic spasm, a tendency to mucus at the top of the wind pipe, which being repeatedly removed in the ordinary way, the last symptom disappears, and the lungs and throat resume their normal condition."

One can become allergic not only to cats, but to other animals like horse, fur-bearing and feather-bearing animals. A thorough history of the patient gives a clue to diagnosis. As in other forms of allergy, here also, it should be understood that a person may have come in contact with a cat, dog or horse and never had symptoms, but may develop them now without any apparent reason. So the argument of the patient that, "I have always kept a cat, without getting any symptoms" does not carry weight.

Exposure to animal allergens in a person who is already allergic to house dust, may lead to an increase of symptoms. In a similar manner, removal of animal allergens may lessen symptoms.

The general rule in treatment of allergy: *Avoid the allergenic agent*, applies here as well. This applies not only to the offending animal in the house, but also to the animals in the houses of other people.

Getting rid of pets is not easy. And so is the case with allergic symptoms if you continue keeping the offending animal.

9

Conditions that Influence Asthma

Bronchial asthma is a common condition; it is estimated that roughly one per cent of the world population have bronchial asthma. Its incidence is a little more in boys than in girls; in adult life, this difference disappears. Incidence is high or even slightly more, in the upper income groups than in the lower.

Influence of Heredity

Asthma occurs more often in person who have a family history of the disease. The greater the degree of inheritance, the greater the likelihood of the off springs becoming sensitive. Furthermore, when both the parents are affected, the disease in the children appears earlier, and often before puberty.

One inherits an allergic predisposition rather than a specific allergic disease; children of a parent suffering from hay fever may develop asthma or eczema and not necessarily hay fever.

Influence of Infection

It has been observed that, many a time, after a throat infection, a child becomes breathless, has wheezy sound in the chest and presents a clinical picture of asthma. When the infection subsides, the chest returns to normal condition. Such symptoms may recur afterwards.

Childhood infections, such as measles, pneumonia, whooping cough or infection in the tonsils and adenoids can set up symptoms of asthma in an already predisposed child.

At times, infection makes an allergy-prone individual to start getting symptoms of allergy. A pre-existing sensitivity to a specific allergen may become manifest in the presence of infection. Once such a sensitivity is activated, it may continue even after the infection is over.

Patients of allergic rhinitis and asthma have excessive secretions from the nose and the lungs. These secretions are excellent medium for the growth of micro-organisms, so that rhinitis and asthma patients are more liable to chest infections.

Thus we see that allergy and infection set up a vicious circle in which each aggravates the other, and the infected asthma patient develops chronic bronchitis and emphysema more often than one with asthma alone. Treatment of both the conditions side by side—infection with proper antibiotics, and allergy with appropriate anti-allergic measures—can ensure early recovery.

Influence of Emotional States

A Case History: While a young girl was working in the kitchen, the gas stove burst and she died from the burns she suffered. On that very day, her mother developed asthma which continued for ten days and then gradually abated.

There is a history of allergy in her family; her father and one of her brothers have eczema. This lady now invariably gets asthma attacks when she hears news related, or in any way similar to the circumstances of her first attack.

Any excessive emotional reaction is known to, sometimes, precipitate an attack of asthma in a person who is already predisposed to it. It has been observed that some asthmatic children when sent to hostels show an improvement in their symptoms. This, among other things, may be due to the child being rid of the emotional problems that surround him at home.

Influence of Climate

Generally speaking, a dry climate is better suited to an asthmatic than a humid one; he feels better away from a sea coast than near it.

Rainy weather, with its increased humidity, is troublesome to some asthmatics. But patients who are allergic to pollens feel better after the rain, as all the pollens present in the air get washed down. The same thing happens in an industrial area having air pollution because most of the pollutants get washed down.

A dry climate, however, is no panacea for the asthmatic, as there are many other factors that come into the picture.

Asthma patients allergic to some pollens develop their symptoms or find them to be aggravated in the early hours of the morning. This is because the flowers of some plants open and discharge their pollens with the first rays of sunlight.

Winds: Some patients experience difficulty when a wind from a particular direction starts blowing. It is probable that the wind picks up pollens in its path, to which the patient is sensitive and when the patient is exposed to it, he gets the symptoms of asthma.

Barometric Pressure: A sudden drop in barometric pressure, as happens immediately before a thunderstorm, is unsuitable to an asthma patient. Some asthmatics and sinusitis patients are so sensitive to this fall in barometric pressure that they can foretell the coming of storms on the basis of the symptoms that they get even when there are no obvious indications.

Altitude: It has been observed that many asthma patients do not develop symptoms when they go to hill stations. It seems that the improvement in the symptoms of these patients is not so much due to the high altitude, as it is to (1) changed environment, (2) changed plants and pollens and (3) lessened dust, in particular, house dust. Mites, the allergenic factor in house dust, grow slowly at the lower temperatures of the hill stations.

Influence of Occupation

Some occupations are particularly hazardous for people with an allergic background or for those who have some manifestations of allergy already in them, as for example asthma. Farmers, poultry-men, dairy workers and bakers are exposed to large amounts of fungus spores. Gardeners, farmers and farm labourers are exposed to a large number of pollens; upholsterers and mattress renovators are exposed to large quantities of house dust; flour-mill workers and carpenters are exposed to various kinds of dusts; beauticians, barbers or furriers are exposed to excessive amounts of animal dander.

For a patient who already has asthma, such occupations may lead to an aggravation of the symptoms. But if a patient has an allergic background and no manifestations of allergy yet, exposure to excessive amounts of pollens, dusts and moulds because of a particular occupation, may lead to the appearance of symptoms of allergy.

Asthma, however, rarely develops after the initial contact with an offending agent. Usually there is a sensitization period of months or even years before any allergic manifestation appears. One asthma patient who came under my observation had symptoms only when he was in his shop; as soon as he came back home, he had no symptoms. He dealt in footwear and was found to be sensitive to leather dust. As soon as somebody cleaned the floor of his shop, he developed symptoms of asthma.

There are certain occupations which cause allergic manifestations not only in the workers but also in people who live in the surrounding area. Such occupations are a public health problem. An epidemic of castor seed allergy in a town occurred, the source of which was a factory extracting castor oil from the castor seed. The process had been carried on for 18 months when the first definite case of castor seed asthma was diagnosed in a factory worker. The epidemic proper began in the following year, when the factory started to discharge waste products into the atmosphere and cases began to be reported among people living or working in the surrounding area or

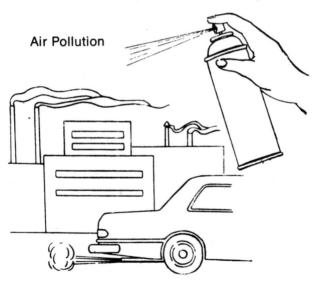

Air Pollution

in the direction of the prevailing wind. Of the 32 patients examined, 22 gave positive reactions to patch tests with castor seed extract. Only 3 of the 32 patients worked in the factory, all the rest lived or worked nearby. The symptoms were varied and usually multiple, including asthma (19 cases), hay fever (18), symptoms such as irritation, redness, swelling and running of the eyes and skin rashes. Attacks generally ceased when the patient left the area. Asthmatics or those who have a strong family history of allergy, must take care while choosing a profession for themselves.

10

Diagnosis of Asthma

A thorough history of the patient of breathlessness is absolutely essential in order to find out whether he is a case of asthma; what he is allergic to; when and what symptoms started first; in which season the symptoms were aggravated; and what are the substances which bring on the attack. Laboratory tests correlated with the case history, help in finding the allergenic factors.

Skin Tests

The skin tests detect the presence of antibodies (reagins) which are present not only in the blood but also in the skin. The union of the antibody in the skin with its corresponding antigen applied in the skin tests, causes the release of histamine or histamine-like substance by the tissues and results in a weal and redness around the test site.

Preparation of Extracts

Skin tests are done with the extracts of the pollens,

dusts, moulds, etc., and it is essential that the extracts be prepared in a proper manner, and that they are active and potent, and not old. Furthermore, they should have no pathogenic micro-organisms in them and have a least amount of any irritant. The more natural characteristics the antigen extract retains, the greater the precision and accuracy of the test results.

For optimum extraction, crude antigens are reduced into a fine powder. This is treated first with ether or acetone to remove fats and oils and then treated with a watery solvent. The resultant is then dialized. Some of the extract is then concentrated and its pH checked and brought to neutral. After sterilization, the extract is then standardized. This is now ready for use.

With this extract, skin tests are done by either of the two techniques: 1) Scratch test and 2) Intracutaneous test.

Scratch Tests: A series of superficial scratches or abrasions about 1/4 cm long are made on the cleansed skin of the arm or the forearm. Over these scratches, which should not be deep enough to cause bleeding, allergenic extracts are applied. After fifteen to twenty minutes, these are removed from the skin, and the reactions at the test sites are observed and interpreted on the basis of comparison with control tests which have been made with diluents devoid of the allergenic principle.

Intracutaneous Tests: These involve the introduction into the skin by a syringe of about 0.02 ml of each of the sterile allergenic extracts. The reactions resulting from the intracutaneous technique are generally larger than those obtained with the scratch technique, and the standards of recording and interpretation vary with each procedure. Intracutaneous tests, if not performed with care, can sometimes cause allergic reactions. The tests themselves are not painful. They are performed even in children who soon lose their apprehension.

The skin test reactions are graded from 0, 1, 2, 3, to 4 plus depending upon the degree of swelling and redness produced. A positive reaction of significance, must correlate with the clinical history of the patient.

Grading of Skin Test

Grade	Size of Weal	Size of Redness
0	Same as control	Same as control
1 +	2 times more than control	10-20 mm
2 +	3 times more than the control	20-30 mm
3 +	4 times more than the control	More than 30 mm
4 +	5 times or more than the control	More than 40 mm

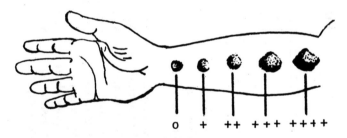

Grading of Skin Tests

Negative reactions normally indicate the absence of antibody against the allergen tested, but other consideterions, such as the use of inadequate, weak, or deteriorated extracts, can account for them.

Skin Testing Chart

Name of the Patient.................

Allergens: English name	Local name	Months in which present in Delhi air	Grading 0 1+ 2+ 3+ 4+
1 POLLENS			
Grasses:			
1. Cenchrus	*Aujan*	July to Oct.	
2. Cynoden	*Doob*	Year round	
3. Pennisetum	*Bajra*	Aug. to Sept.	
4. Sorghum	*Jawar*	Aug. to Sept.	
Weeds:			
1. Adhatoda	*Rusa*	Dec. to Jan.	
2. Ageratum	*Neelum*	Dec. to Apr.	
3. Amaranthus spinosus	*Kately* *Chauli*	Year round	
4. Argemone	*Peeli Kateli*	Jan. to Mar.	
5. Artemisia		Sept. to Oct.	
6. Asphodelous	*Piazi*	Jan. to Mar.	
7. Brassica	*Sarson*	Dec. to Mar.	
8. Cannabis		Feb. to Mar.	

Allergens English name	Local name	Months in which present in Delhi air	Grading 0 1 + 2 + 3 + 4 +
Indica	Bhang	July to Sept.	
9. Chenopodium album	Bathuva	Dec. to Mar.	
10. Dodonea	Vilaiti mehndi	Jan. to Feb.	
11. Parthenium		*Year round*	
12. Xanthium	Chhota gokhru	Sept. & Apr.	
Trees:		Aug. to Feb.	
1. Cassia siamea	Safeda	May to Oct.	
2. Eucalyptus	Zarphanoos	Apr. to May	
3. Kigelia	Bakain	Mar.	
4. Melia	Shahtoot	Feb. to Mar.	
5. Morus	Vilaiti	Mar. to April	
6. Prosopis	Kikkar	Sept. to Nov.	
7. Putranjiva		Apr.	

Allergens: English name	Local name	Months in which present in Delhi air	Grading 0 1+ 2+ 3+ 4+
8. Ricinus	*Arandi*	Year round	
9. Salvadora	*Peelu*	Nov. to Mar.	
II DUSTS			
1. House dust			
2. Paper dust			
3. Wheat dust			
4. Cotton dust			
III FUNGI			
1. Alternaria		Year round	
2. *Aspergillus fumigatus*		Sept. to Nov.	
3. Candida		May to Nov.	
4. Cladosporium		Sept. to Nov.	
5. Helminthosporium		Feb. to June	
6. Mucor		May to Oct.	
7. Phoma		Oct. & Nov.	
IV DANDERS			
1. Horse			
2. Dog			
3. Cat			

Do's & Don'ts for Asthma Patients

Do's

- Get up in the morning at a regular hour.
- Take morning walks or do some physical exercise.
- Take simple diet without spices at regular hours. Discretion in diet should be strictly observed.
- Keep your bed-room clean of dust. It should have no rugs or carpets in it.
- Take your medicine regularly as directed by your doctor.
- Always maintain regularity in your dialy work routine.
- Always sleep early at night at regular hours to get up early.

Dont's

- Do not disturb your physical as well as mental activities of your daily routine.
- Try to avoid smoking completely.
- Hard drinks should be avoided.
- Do not over eat as it is prone to asthma attack.
- Keep yourself away from smoke and dust.
- Keep your room pollution-free.

Provocation Inhalation Tests: In order to a confirm doubtful positive skin reaction some doctors perform provocative inhalation tests. The extract which was doubtfully positive, is given to the patient to inhale and it is seen whether the patient gets breathless after it or not. The spasm of the airways produced as a result of positive reaction is measured by making the patient take a breath test called spirometry.

When combined with skin test information, this test has the potential of providing valuable data about the causative allergen. However, this test is never safe, and in some patients precipitates severe attack of asthma. Hence this test is never done outside a well-equipped hospital which can handle respiratory emergencies.

11

Treating Asthma by Drugs

Asthma is treated firstly, to remove or lessen its symptoms and agony, and secondly, to remove its cause as far as possible. It is better and desirable that both aspects be undertaken side by side. Let us first take the drug treatment of asthma.

As we have already seen, a patient of asthma during an attack has narrowing of the airways and excessive production of lung secretions. The narrowed airways make respiration and exchange of gases in the lungs difficult, so that the patient has less of the oxygen and more of carbon dioxide in his blood.

The excessive secretions can within a short while lead to infection in the lungs, as the secretions are the nutrients of the different kind of bacteria and they grow very fast on it.

Furthermore, since a patient having an attack of asthma breathes very fast, he loses lot of water in the air which he throws out, and so loses, a lot of water from his body.

Treatment During an Attack

1. If the attack is very severe and prolonged, leading to deficiency of oxygen in the blood, which can be clinically ascertained by looking for bluish tinge on the body, tongue or conjunctivae, then administration of oxygen through nose is called for.
2. The narrowing of the airways has to be removed and production of excessive secretion stopped.
3. If there are signs of infection in the lungs, appropriate antibiotics are to be given.
4. If the patient is dehydrated, intravenous 5 per cent glucose-saline is to be given.

Let us take up these items in more detail. Giving of Theophylline tablets (100 mg each), 2 tablets twice or thrice a day, depending upon the age, weight and severity of the condition, proves very helpful. Theophylline-Retard or sustained action tablets are also available.

The simplest and the well-tried drug combination for causing dilatation of the airways is giving a tablet which contains ephedrine, aminophylline and phenobarbitone. This combination is available under different proprietory names such as Tedral, Franal etc. This can be repeated two or three times a day. For children, syrups are available containing this combination.

For most patients having mild or moderate attack of asthma, this proves very helpful and even adequate in itself. Some patients do complain of palpitation after taking these tablets, and older patients having high blood pressure have to take it in lesser quantities. Ephedrine in it can cause constipation and if the patient has some enlargement of the prostate, it can cause some difficulty in passing urine. But generally speaking, such tablets prove very efficacious.

Drugs like salbutamol (which are B-2 stimulators) have come into use lately. They specifically dilate the bronchial airways without excessively stimulating the heart, so that they do not usually lead to palpitation. These drugs come in the form of tablets, injections or aerosol inhalers. In combination with deriphylline, salbutamol tablets prove very useful.

In case there is a severe attack of asthma, deriphylline injection given intramuscularly or aminophylline with 5 per cent glucose intravenously, slowly in 5 to 10 minutes proves helpful. Aminophylline (0.24 gm or double its dose) given through intravenous drip with 5 per cent glucose is very useful. An injection of adrenaline (1 : 1000 solution) 1/2 ml, given very slowly subcutaneously, is also effective in many cases.

Most patients usually need only this medication and care. But, at times, the symptoms increase or when an infection supervenes, extra care is needed. If bacterial infection is present in the respiratory passages and unless properly and adequately treated, bron-chodilator drugs either exert diminished action or have no action at all, so that the patient keeps getting breathless. So, as far as possible, the causative organism must be identified, its sensitiveness to a drug found, and then the proper drug administered.

But in the majority of the cases, this is not possible either because of the lack of facilities or the procedure takes more time than a patient can afford. In such a situation, ampicillin has been found to be helpful: one or two capsules of 250 mg thrice a day for a week proves adequate; the dose and length of adminis-tration depends, however, upon the severity of infection.

If the attack of asthma is such that it is not controlled by the bronchodilator tablets, injections as well as the antibiotics, then the patient can be put on corticos-teroids. These can be given as tablets or intramuscularly or in very severe cases, intravenously.

Treatment in Status Asthmaticus

If the patient has been in status asthmaticus (i.e., continuous and severe attack of asthma for more than

24 hours), it is important to keep in mind that he may also be dehydrated because of excessive loss of water from the lungs; by excessive perspiration and by omitting to take fluids while in an attack. Hence his fluid loss has to be replaced adequately. This, besides restoring the fluid balance of the body, lessens the thickness of the tenacious sputum so that it is coughed out easily. In such a case, intravenous fluids are administered early, usually 3 to 5 litres in the first twenty-four hour period, and thereafter 3 litres daily until hydration is achieved. Fluids usually consist of 5 per cent dextrose in water; every second or third such fluid should contain sodium chloride, particularly if prolonged intravenous therapy is necessary, or if the patient is perspiring freely and he vomits or has diarrhoea. As the patient becomes hydrated and starts eating well, the intravenous administration of fluids can be curtailed.

A cyanosed patient of asthma in status asthmaticus is in need of oxygen which must be given. This can be given either through a catheter in the nose or through a ventri-mask or through a positive pressure breathing apparatus along with a bronchodilator; the last mode of therapy has proved to be more effective.

The use of expectorants in the management of asthma is one of the most important yet often neglected aspects of treatment. One of the best expectorants is potassium iodide; when it is tolerated poorly, other substances such as glyceral guiacolate and ammonium chloride may be useful. Water vapour also may be helpful in thinning bronchial secretions.

Patients with severe asthma become profoundly exhausted, lose sleep, experience increasing anxiety, and therefore, are in need of a tranquilliser, but it should be kept to a minimum, because excess of it can interfere with respiration.

Deaths from asthma can occur in spite of the antibiotics and steroids. These occur not only in older people who die of the complications of long-standing asthma, but also in younger people aged between 5 and 35 years. Majority of these deaths occur outside the hospital. These are due to the fact that the patient and his relations could not realise the severity of the situation.

A proper understanding of the patient's fears and anxieties and the allaying of these fears through sympathetic conversation helps asthma patients very much. The majority of these patients are prone to suggestion. It has been seen, time and again, that when a prescription is given or a line of treatment is started with the emphatic suggestion to the patient that this will definitely give relief, it decidedly works and the patient fulfils the expectations. Not only that, I have observed, that with whatever symptoms the patient may come, a word from the doctor that the patient looks better, produces a corresponding response and the hope given that "You will improve still further", works miracle. Such an approach is helpful, but care must be taken because over-optimistic hopes, once shattered, cause more harm than good.

Aerosol Inhalers

Aerosol are the solid or liquid particles of a substance suspended in air. They are very small, less than a micron (1/1000 mm) in size.

Aerosol inhalers were used initially with bronchodilator drugs like Isoprenaline. But because this drug caused many side-effects such as palpitation and dizziness and some deaths too due to too frequent use, this mode of treatment fell into some disrepute.

With the availability of aerosol inhalers with salbutamol and corticosteroids, this form of treatment has become now very popular.

The technique of using the inhaler is as follows:

1. Shake the inhaler. Remove the cap from its

mouth-piece. Insert the mouth-piece in the lips and purse the lips tightly around it.

2. Take one or two breaths with the inhaler in the mouth.

3. Exhale completely, and then as you start inhaling, press the nozzle-button of the inhaler. Aerosol would go in the airways alongwith the air inhaled.

4. Now remove the inhaler from the mouth. Keep the lips closed, and hold the breath as long as possible, then open the mouth.

5. You can repeat the process and take one more dose of aerosol from the inhaler. The dose that comes out each time on pressing the inhaler is equal and is measured.

Controversy about Cortisone

Cortisone, the miracle drug, has provided renewed hopes to the patients suffering from very severe forms of allergies including asthma. This is a very potent drug and ought to be used in acute life-threatening situations. In asthma cases, cortisone can help patients where nothing else helps, but then it ought to be used only when everything else has been tried and has failed.

It is difficult to say which manifestation of allergy are helped the most, but it is the asthma patients who make maximum use of them.

Among the asthma patients, corticosteroids have provided the maximum and most-needed relief to those having status asthmaticus. Intramuscular or intravenous administration abolishes symptoms in those patients in whom adrenaline or aminophylline have not been of much use. After corticosteroid administration, some of the patients who previously did no respond to adrenaline or aminophylline start responding and once the attack has subsided, oral administration can be resorted to. Gradually, the corticosteroids can be tapered off and the patient can be put on other routine bronchodilators.

Short term use of corticosteroids has proved very helpful to those asthma patients who do not do well with the usual bronchodilators or to those who do not get adequate relief from them.

With the dosage and time for which these drugs are usually prescribed, no serious side effects or complications are observed. Complaints of general weakness or epigastric distress or diminished appetite are certainly not more than are encountered when patients are given ephedrine and aminophylline.

Acute attacks not responding to other routine measures, show excellent improvement in seasonal asthma cases. On the other hand, perennial asthmatic cases who have developed irreversible structural changes in the lungs, do not respond very well.

Care in Administration: The conditions generally forbid the use of cortisone are diabetes mellitus, peptic ulcer, gastrointestinal bleeding, tuberculosis, psychosis, old age, chronic kidney disease, heart attack and significant hypertension. However, these contraindications are more relative than absolute. Long-term taking of corticosteroids may produce hairiness (hirsutism) over the face.

While corticosteroids are being taken, an acute infection in the body does not produce as much symptoms as it would do otherwise. Hence, if the symptoms of an infection are even minor, a doctor ought to be consulted.

Upon discontinuation of the corticosteroids, or on a too rapid decrease dosage, some patients complain of tiring easily, weakness, nervousness, irritability, gastro-intestinal disturbances and occasional dizziness.

Cortisone Inhaler: In cases of intractable asthma where other medications have failed or have not provided adequate relief and cortisone tablets have to be taken, cortisone inhaler reduces the need for the tablets. Since the inhaled cortisone acts locally in the lungs, it hardly produces any side-effects. The inhaler is needed to be used 3 to 4 times a day and provides appreciable relief.

Inhalations of cortisone in heavy dosage and for long periods can lead to growth of fungi in the throat, causing soreness and discomfort. If it happens, the inhalations have to be stopped.

Sodium Cromoglycate: Its Role in Treatment

Sodium cromoglycate is derived from the leaves of a plant, initially used by asthma patients in Eygpt. Researches led to extraction of the active principle, sodium cromoglycate which was later on synthesized and is now available under the company's name of Intal and other brand names.

Sodium cromoglycate is neither a bronchodilator like ephedrine, nor a corticosteroid or an antihistamine. It action is unique; when inhaled as fine powder, it coats the respiratory mucous membrane. Now if an allergic person inhales an allergic agent like pollens which go and settle on the cells to which is attached the antibodies, it prevents the release of histamine and other products from inside the mast cells because it makes the cell wall strong and stable. When these products are not released, the patient suffers no symptoms of allergy even when exposed to the allergens.

Inhalation of sodium cromoglycate prevents the occurrence of asthmatic attacks. The effect of a single inhalation stays for four to six hours, after which the drug disintegrates. Repeat inhalation three to four times a day, can act as prophylactic against an attack of asthma.

Cromoglycate particles are inhaled in a special gadget, the *spinhaler*. It has two parts: the main body with a gray sleeve and a mouth-piece with the propeller. Cromoglycate comes in the capsule. The capsule is inserted with its coloured end downward, into the propeller. The body of the spinhaler is screwed into the mouth piece and the gray sleeve is moved down once and then brought up. This act pierces the capsule for the powder to come out. Spinhaler is held in the hand and breath is exhaled as much as possible. Now tilting the head back, mouth-piece is placed between the teeth and lips pursed around it, and then a quick deep breath is taken in. Breath is held for sometime, and then exhaled through the nose. The whole process of breathing in is repeated once or twice. Then the spinhaler is removed from the mouth and checked for the total emptiness of the capsule.

Corticosteroid-dependent asthmatics are mostly able to reduce to smaller dosage levels with added Intal, or sometimes stop taking the drug altogether. Analysis of patients receiving Intal for periods of upto 12 months has shown no significant long-term side effects and no real evidence of the development of Intal-dependence, but in some cases loss in the efficacy of the drug after some months has been seen.

Sodium cromoglycate has very little value, if any, in the immediate relief of a severe asthma attack and certainly has no place in the emergency treatment of established status asthmaticus. Its effect is only preventive, not curative.

Antihistamines in Asthma

Antihistamines are not effective in the case of asthma in adults. They have no effect on bronchospasm; in fact, the symptoms sometimes get aggravated because of the drying up of the secretions and the subsequent difficulty in passing phlegm. Allergic cough in children, however, is helped by giving antihistamines along with a bronchodilator in cough mixture.

Any drug taken should be in consultation with your doctor.

12

Treating Asthma by Hyposensitization Injections

If you are a patient of asthma, the first thing to be established from the history of your disease is, whether you could be having allergy as the major basis of your disease. If that is established, then the next is: to what your are allergic. After this has been done with the help of skin tests etc. two things need to be done, in order of preference: 1) to avoid the things to which you are allergic; 2) if you are allergic to things such as pollens, moulds etc. that are present in the air and cannot be avoided, then you must be made resistant to them. This is done by a process variously known as *hyposensitization or immunotherapy.* In this process, the patient is injected with gradually increasing dose and concentrations of the extracts of the substances to which he is sensitive.

Procedure

The preparation of these extracts has already been described. We shall now have a look at the procedures for giving the injections. There are three methods of hyposensitization: pre-seasonal, co-seasonal, and perennial.

Pre-seasonal: This is started three to four months prior to the onset of the season in which the patient gets the symptoms. Injections are usually given according to a schedule so that the optimum dose is reached before the offending season begins. 15 to 20 injections are usually necessary. Pre-seasonal injections may be terminated at the onset of the season if the patient has already improved adequately, or treatment may be continued during the season (co-seasonally). During the season, however, dosage is sharply reduced, because the patient is inhaling considerable amounts of pollens etc. from the atmosphere as well, and it is possible for the treatment to aggravate the symptoms rather than lessening them. The maximum dose tolerated during the season should be reduced by 30 to 50 per cent or more, or discontinued completely, if there is any suspicion of causing an increase in symptoms.

Co-seasonal: Co-seasonal injections are given to those patients who present themselves just prior to or during the pollen season. It is advisable to use very dilute pollen extracts and not to attempt to reach any sizable dose too soon.

Perennial: This consists of continuation of hyposensitization even after the aggravating season. The injections are given all round the year; however the interval between them is increased more and more.

Schedule of Injections

To begin with, a 1 : 5,000 dilution of the allergens to which a patient is sensitive, is given bi-weekly injections, starting with 0.1 ml and then increasing by 0.1 ml each time till a 0.9 ml dose is reached.

If the patient has had no reactions with dose and concentration, then the next course is started and the concentration of the extracts increased ten times, i.e., 1 : 500, and weekly injections of that are given, starting with 0.1 ml and reaching 0.9 ml.

The third course of injections begins with a 1 : 50 concentration of the allergens and the injections are given starting with 0.1 ml and going upto 0.15 ml. Thereafter seven more weekly injections of 0.5 ml are given, keeping the concentrations of the extracts the same, i.e., 1 : 50 which is the maximum concentration. The procedure adopted for further injections is given on page 76 and 77.

Modifications in this schedule of injections and dosage are practised by different doctors depending upon their own experience with the allergen extracts they use.

Some patients, as a result of the injection, complain of an aggravation of their symptoms for a day or so. If the aggravation of symptoms is unbearable, the dose of the injections is reduced. Sometimes, a swelling or urticarial patches appear at the site of injection; this also calls for a lessening of the dose. Since most reactions occur soon after the injection, it is better that the patient sits for some time in the clinic so that proper observations can be made and remedial measures taken if necessary.

The perennial method of hyposensitization carries a slightly higher incidence of constitutional reactions; on the other hand, most doctors believe that the relief obtained is much greater with perennial therapy than with either seasonal or co-seasonal injections.

Results

Assessments of the results of hyposensitization have been done by different doctors. The results reported vary from total cures in a large percentage of cases to other not so beneficial results.

The efficacy of hyposensitization therapy is very difficult to evaluate accurately because there are so many variables involved. The lack of uniformity in the preparation of pollen extracts, the variation in dosage schedules, and the lack of a standard for estimating the degree of relief obtained, render it difficult to arrive at accurate statistics.

The commonest causes of failure are the use of improper pollen extracts because of an incorrect clinical diagnosis, the employment of stale, deteriorated extracts which have not been kept under refrigeration, overdosage or underdosage, and the failure to recognize and control other non-pollen allergies which the patient may have.

Mode of Action

It is now known with certainty how hyposensitization achieves its results. At one stage, it was thought that blocking antibodies against the extracts to which the patient is allergic, are produced as a result of hyposensitization. But it has been noticed that the degree of improvement in symptoms and the level of the blocking antibodies do not go hand in hand.

Antigen-Injection Mixture

This is prepared according to the allergy skin test results of the individual, and is special for each patient. The injections are given in the upper arm under the skin, the dose and concentration of each injection is according to the directions of the prescribing doctor.

Before the injection is given, it is necessary for the patient as well as the nurse/doctor to recognize the vial properly. After taking the injection, the patient should remain in the doctor's clinic for about 20 minutes to check for any adverse side effects.

If change occurs in colour or consistency of the injection material in the bottle, or a precipitation forms, this must be reported to the doctor. It is possible that such a change is due to bacteria entering into the bottle when the needle is inserted into it to withdraw the injection material.

Prescription Chart for Hyposensitization

Name of the patient................   Date................

Pollen Quantity	1. Cenchrus	2. Cynoden	3. Pennisetum	4. Sorghum
Pollen Quantity	5. Adhatoda	6. Ageratum	7. Amaranthus spinosus	8. Argemone
Pollen Quantity	9. Chenopodiun album	10. Dodonea	11. Parthenium	12. Xanthium
Pollen Quantity	13. Cassia siamea	14. Eucalyptus	15. Kigelia	16. Melia
Pollen Quantity	17. Morus	18. Prosopis	19. Putranjiva	20. Ricinus
Pollen Quantity	21. Salvadora			

Dusts	22. House dust	23. Paper dust	24. Wheat dust	25. Cotton dust
Quantity				
Fungi	26. Alter naria	27. Asp. fumg.	28 Candida	29 Cladosporium
Quantity				
Fungi	30. Helminthos-porium	31. Mucor	32. Phoma	
Quantity				
Dander	Horse	34. Dog	35. Cat	

Vials

(I) 1 : 5000 (II) 1 : 500 (III) 1 : 50

The injection vial is kept in the refrigerator but not frozen. Ordinary room temperature lessens its potency. In the absence of a refrigerator, it can be kept in a thermos flask after putting the vial in a polythene bag and tying the top of it with a string or rubber band, so that the water does not touch the bottle.

Regularity in taking the injections according to schedule is necessary, otherwise the benefit drawn would be less and likelihood of reactions greater. If some injections are missed due to unavoidable causes, the doctor must be informed of it, so that he can decide the dose-schedule again.

There is no evidence to suggest that these injections cannot be taken during pregnancy. However, the obstetrician should be consulted in this regard.

Some amount of redness and swelling around the site of injection is not uncommon. This local reaction lasts a short while. If it causes troublesome itching, a tablet of antihistamine would help. Inform the doctor the next time you visit him about it.

Hyposensitization Chart

Name....................   Date......................

Date	Dose and its concentration	Patient's condition	Drugs taken
	I) *1:5000*		
	0.1 ml		
	0.2 ml		
	0.3 ml		
	0.4 ml		
	0.5 ml		
	0.6 ml		
	0.7 ml		
	0.8 ml		
	0.9 ml		
	II) *1:500* [1]		
	0.1 ml		
	0.2 ml		
	0.3 ml		
	0.4 ml		
	0.5 ml		
	0.6 ml		
	0.7 ml		
	0.8 ml		
	0.9 ml		

1 . Subcutaneous injections, *twice* a week

Date	Dose and its concentration	Patient's condition	Drugs taken
	III) *1:50* [2]		
	0.1 ml		
	0.2 ml		
	0.3 ml		
	0.4 ml		
	0.5 ml		
	0.5 ml		
	0.5 ml		
	0.5 ml		
	0.5 ml		
	0.5 ml		
	0.5 ml		
	0.5 ml		
	IV) *1:50* [3]		
	0.6 ml		
	0.6 ml		
	0.6 ml		
	0.6 ml		
	0.6 ml		
	0.6 ml		
	0.6 ml		
	0.6 ml		

[2] S/C injections, *once* a week

[3] S/C injections; *once* in *two* weeks

Date	Dose and its concentration	Patient's condition	Drugs taken
	V) *1:50* [4]		
	0.7 ml		
	0.7 ml		
	0.7 ml		
	0.7 ml		
	0.7 ml		
	0.7 ml		
	0.7 ml		
	VI) *1:50* [5]		
	0.8 ml		
	0.8 ml		
	0.8 ml		
	0.8 ml		
	0.8 ml		
	0.8 ml		

[4] S/C injections; *once* in 3 weeks

[5] S/C injections, *once* in 4 weeks

Note: Continue 0.8 ml injections after every 4 weeks for up to a total period of two years of hyposensitization from the start of the treatment

Instructions for the Patient and the Treating Doctor during Hyposensitization

1. Note the concentration of the antigen mixture in each bottle provided to you carefully. The first lot usually has three bottles: I) 1: 5000, (II) 1: 500, III) 1: 50. Use No. I—1: 5000 first. After this is finished, then use No. II—I: 500, and then No. III—1: 50.

2. Keep the bottles in a refrigerator. Do not freeze the contents.

3. Shake the bottle before giving the injection.

4. Use Tuberculin Syringe, and Hypodermic needle No. 26 or 27 gauze.

5. Give subcutaneous injection. Suck the needle before injecting the material to see the blood does not enter it. If it does, change the site.

6. Stick to the dosage schedule.

7. Fill up the form provided wherever indicated each time the injection is given.

8. A small swelling about a centimeter or so with redness around it is normal. If the swelling and redness is much larger, and there is itching at the injection site, take an antihistamine tablet (25 mg Avil tablet). This will help in the quick disappearance of the symptoms.

9. Reduce the dose of the injection if the previous one was troublesome.

10. Wait in the doctor's clinic for half an hour, after the injection.

11. Local reactions are not uncommon, but general reactions are rare.

    However if a general reaction occurs within a few minutes to half an hour after the injection (symptoms such as urticaria, beginning or aggravation of asthmatic symptoms, or gasping and collapse or shock), proceed as follows:

a) Tie a tourniquet above the site of injection.

b) Give injection adrenaline 1/2 ml subcutaneously slowly in the other arm.

c) Also give an injection of antihistamine Avil/ Phanergan 1/m or 1/v or in the drip.

d) Give Decadron injection 1/m or 1/v or in the drip

e) Give oxygen intranasally through the catheter.

12. If the colour of the injection material becomes muddy after 3-4 injections, and there develops a fever in the patient within 24 hours after the injection, it is likely that the antigen-material has been infected with outside bacteria. Discard the bottle, and request for a new one.

13

Diet for Asthma Patients

Proper diet taken at regular times is very important for a patient of asthma. This can not only prevent an attack from occurring but also can lessen the severity of the attack that a patient is having.

The diet should be light, nutritious and well balanced. It should not contain such things which don't go well with the patient. Experience shows that for north Indians, rice taken at night causes discomfort in breathing. This may be because of the fact that to satisfy hunger with rice, one has to take a large quantity of it, so that the stomach is bloated and this puts hindrance in the way of the full and proper working of the diaphragm in respiration. Other things that patients generally complain of not being comfortable to them are taking of bananas; among the vegetables ladyfingers and among the lentil, *urad* and its *dal*. So these may be avoided. Spices should be avoided in diet. With some people, cold drinks and sour preparations like *chuttnies* and pickles cause more coughing; so these may be avoided.

Asthma patient should not take full-stomach meal. Fulness of stomach after meals—in particular at night causes discomfort in breathing or even precipitates breathlessness. One should take less quantity at a time, though he may take for more number of times. Fried things should be avoided as far as possible.

No sweet dish should be taken at night. A patient of asthma would notice that he feels more comfortable during the night if at the time of sleep his stomach is not heavy. So dinner should be taken at least two hours before one goes to bed.

Asthma patient should take more of vegetables, cheese, eggs and chiken, soups and fruits. But all of these should be taken in moderation. There should be adequate variety in the diet of the patient so that he does not feel bored with it.

It is preferable that an asthma patient avoids taking food outside his house, particularly the party dishes; they are all heavy with fat and frying. However, in order to avoid attention towards oneself, one may, if it is possible, take lighter meal than usual with one or two innocuous looking dishes.

Diet for Children

Children who develop asthma do not pick up weight or even lose weight. So special attention has to be given to their diet.

A child requires more calories per kilogram of body weight than an adult, because 1) his basal metabolic rate is higher, 2) he indulges in greater physical activity, and 3) more calories are needed by him for the growth of his body. An asthmatic child has even greater metabolic rate, because of hurried breathing.

So the child needs more carbohydrates and more proteins. If the diet is otherwise well balanced, no extra addition of minerals and vitamins are necessary

A liberal amount of water should be given to child asthmatics, because they lose a lot of it in respiration. Meal hours should be regular, and as far as possible, nibbling in between meals should not be allowed.

A child may be told what he should not take as for example, pickles, *chuttnies* etc. He should not, however, be unduly forced to take a particular diet which he does not like. On the other hand, his likes and dislikes should be anticipated and variety introduced in the diet which is well balanced.

If the child is otherwise healthy—eats well, plays well, sleeps well—but does not take adequate food according to the parents standard, then it is parent and not the child who needs to be instructed.

While some children like to live disciplined lives, others don't. There are some children to whom milk-taking day after day is monotonous; for such children, variety in serving milk preparation should be found.

Taking more sweets while keeping the calories adequate in diet, makes it deficient in proteins.

School-going children often hurry through their breakfast because they get up late, and then hurry through their lunch, because they have to play. And then take a heavy dinner. All this is wrong. A full stomach while going to bed is more liable to lead to an attack of asthma during the night.

Diet for Old People

The lessened activity and lowered metabolic rate reduces the calorie requirements. If the patient is also suffering from some other disease like arthritis or angina, the activity is further reduced.

If an older asthmatic is taking corticosteroids occasionally or regularly, then the old age plus the effect of these drugs, leads to weakening of the bones (osteoporosis) because of the deficiency of calcium, protein, vitamins, minerals and hormones. It is not uncommon to find in an X-ray of the chest that one or more of the vertebrae are broken and collapsed. The whole body of an older asthmatic is shrunken—the height, the muscles, the girth of the abdomen.

If the patient has lost weight, calorie content of the diet should be increased. When the patient feels better, he must be asked to take more diet so as to regain weight.

Patient must be asked to take more proteins: milk, cheese, pulses, soyabeans; if he is non-vegetarian, then he can add chicken or its soup, meat, egg and fish, provided he is not allergic to any of these. For the sake of variety in diet, custard, puddings can be taken, particularly so if mastication is the problem because of loss of teeth.

Intake of fat should be limited. Anyone of the multivitamin tablets with mineral should be added to the daily diet.

Injections of one of the anabolic steroids are helpful in older in older people to regain protein retention; some increase in weight and a general feeling of being energised. Decadurabolin injection 1/m once a fortnight has been found to be helpful.

A Suggestied Diet*

Mixed Diet	Vegetarian
On rising	
A glass of warm water, light tea—one cup	A glass of warm water, light tea—one cup
Breakfast	
Egg, half-boiled or scrambled, toast, butter, seasonal fruit	Porridge or corn-flakes with milk and sugar, toast and butter, seasonal fruit
II am	
Fruit juice (orange)—1 cup	Fruit juice (orange)—1 cup
Lunch	
Meat or chicken with boiled potatoes and beans/seasonal vegetables *Chappatis* Custard—1/2 cup	Curd—1 cup Dal—1 cup Cooked vegetables *Chappatis* Custard—1/2 cup
4 pm	
Tea with biscuits	Tea with biscuits Lightly fried cheese
Dinner	
Cooked vegetables *Dal* *Chappatis*	Cooked vegatables *Dal* *Chappatis*

*Its equivalent varieties can be made in many ways.

Food Do's and Dont's

Avoid

...Fried and fatty foods.

...Overloading your stomach

...Smoking.

...Drinking.

...Sweet dish at·night.

...Going out in cold air at night after dinner.

Instead

...Eat simple food without spices at regular hours

...Take light and nourishing food provided one does not have known allergy to any of them.

...Take plenty of water during an attack of asthma.

...Take dinner early in the evening, say 2 hours before sleep.

...Take very light dinner so that the stomach is almost empty when fall asleep.

14

Daily Routine for Asthma Patients

Asthma patients have been observed to feel better and have lesser symptoms on days when they have a regular routine than othewise. Any irregularity in their diet or work or working and sleeping hours affect them badly. *Hence regularity in daily routine is a must in an asthma patient.*

He should get up in the morning at a regular hour. That also means that he go to bed at a regular hour, not too late. It is preferable that he should go for a walk in the morning or do some physical exercise at home. His diet should be simple, and taken at regular hours—small meals at a time.

An asthma patient should not smoke at all. The smoke and the smoky particles, to say the least, are irritant to the respiratory tract, so that the person not only gets more bronchospasm but also is more liable to respiratory infections.

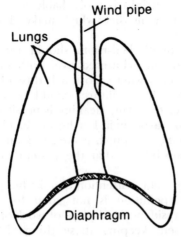

Breathing Out—the Diaphragm at Rest

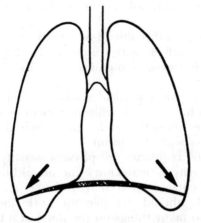

Breathing in—the Diaphragm Flattens

How the Diaphragm Works

Hard drinks should be avoided as far as possible. A person who drinks is more liable to overeat or to get indiscreet in his diet, which makes him prone to asthma attack.

Asthma patient's bed-room should remain only a bed-room, and not cluttered over with other things. It should be such where too much dust or wind does not come in. The furniture should be arranged in such a manner that daily cleaning is possible. It should have no rug or carpet in it. Furthermore, it is preferable if the bed-room is as much protected from extraneous sounds as possible, so that the patient does not get disturbed.

So far as possible, attention should be given to the fact that air pollution is not good for an asthma patient. The residence and place of work or profession may be chosen, keeping these things in view. An asthma patient should avoid outings or picnic in the gardens or countryside in the season in which he has symptoms.

Discretions in diet should be strictly observed in the season in which he gets symptoms. In the months in which he is free of symptoms, some indulgence may be allowed.

When to take a particular tablet or medicine and how much to take, an intelligent patient quickly learns to regulate himself; and he can lessen the need of consultation with the doctor.

Not only regularity in physical activity but also mental activity is mandatory for an asthma patient. Getting mental tension may provoke an attack of asthma. He should not pile up work and decision taking. Too many things on the mind at a time, leads to tension and worry which ought to be avoided.

The essential theme of managing asthma is regularity in daily routine, knowing one's limitations and observing them. The wise patients who observe these rules, most of the time, find that asthma at its worst is only a nuisance.

15

Breathing Exercises for Asthma Patients

In normal breathing, it is diaphragm that does the greatest amount of work: when one inhales, the diaphragm moves downward; when one exhales, the diaphragm moves upward squeezing the air out of the lungs.

The asthma patient, over a period of time, develops an unnatural habit of breathing. During an attack, the tendency for him is to breathe mostly and quickly from the upper part of the chest rather than the whole chest. This makes the chest muscles work hard, particularly so as they are working against constricted airways.

Aims: Breathing exercises aim at:

1. Relaxing the over-worked chest muscles, and
2. Increasing the use of diaphragm and of the abdominal muscle rather than the chest muscles.

In order to achieve the proper working of the diaphragm and lower chest, the asthma patient has *to concentrate on breathing out rather than breathing in.* He has to try to empty his chest and raise the diaphragm by voluntary contraction of the abdomen and 'lower chest, thereby trying to reverse the procedure which exists during an attack of asthma. Furthermore, *breathing out has to· be a slow process* and not a hasty one, otherwise it leads to wheezing and discomfort

In order to break this vicious cycle, it is necessary to retrain the patient in the use of his diaphragm and abdominal muscles. *And the best method for it is that he concentrates all his attention on pushing out his abdomen. This automatically leads to lower chest breathing.*

Practice Breathing Exercises—They Help

Relaxation of Chest Muscles

Relaxation of the body and of the chest muscles form the first stage of this re-training programme. This can be achieved through different positions and exercises.

1. Sit forward with the forearms resting across the thights.

2. Stand with feet apart, the arm raised sideways to a horizontal position, and relax. This exercise is done to a 4-beat rhythm in which the arm is raised during the first two beats and brought down during the next two beats. Let the arm fall loosely so that it drops and the momentum carries it slightly across the body.

   A variation of this is swinging the arm in a circle and carrying it backwards, upwards and forwards.

3. Sit with legs stretched and feet apart, arms hanging relaxedly, on the sides. Breathe out slowly and drop the head until it reaches between the knees. Raise the body gradually until the lower part of the back is straight first, followed by the middle and the upper part of the back and finally the head. Keep breathing in until the starting position is reached. This exercise should be done as slowly as possible. This is called the *forward bending exercise*. Forward bending can also be done in the standing position.

When walking on going up a slope, or upstairs, the patient must be taught to consciously relax his arms and thorax.

In bed, the patient should learn to lie down on one side, with two pillows under the head, the upper arm and legs flexed forward; the upper arm behind and the whole body turned forward.

Older patients, and those with cardiac complications or emphysema find 'high side-lying' on pillows very comfortable. The patient soon learns to arrange them correctly.

Another position, particularly useful in an attack of asthma is to sit and lean forward, with the head and arms resting on pillows, on a table.

In all these positions, there is a forward tilting of the trunk.

Once the relaxation position is assumed, the patient's sequence of thought should ·be relaxation of hands, neck, chest and the maintenance of these while breathing rhythmically with his lower ribs.

Use of Diaphragm and Abdominal Muscles

There are different exercises or positions to achieve this and a relaxed position, if already learnt, can help a great deal:

1. Head of the bed should be raised by 18 inches. Lie with knees drawn up, if this is more comfortable. Breathe in through the nose relaxing the upper part of the chest, pushing the abdomen out and expanding the lower part of the chest. Breathe out slowly through the mouth, gently allowing the chest and the abdomen to sink. Do this 15 to 20 times. Rest for a minute and repeat the exercise for 5 minutes. This is abdominal breathing, with the abdomen moving in and out.

2. Place your hands well up on the sides of the chest to give pressure on the lower ribs. Keep the upper chest and the shoulders relaxed throught the exercise. Breathe out slowly through your mouth while squeezing the ribs with hands·to expel all the air from the lower part of the chest. Take a deep breath and expand the lower part of the chest against the pressure of the hands. Repeat the exercise for 3 minutes. This helps in the expansion of the lower chest on both sides.

   Later, the patient can place his forearms and hands across his lower ribs and with gentle pressure, learn to feel the correct expansion and contraction of his ribs.

3. Stretch the right knee while breathing in and bring the right leg back to the original position while breathing out. Repeat with left knee.

4. Lift the right leg straight up. At the same time take in the breath. Bring the leg slowly down and breathe out. Repeat with left leg.

5. Raise arms over head and expand the lower part of the chest. Bring the arms back in a relaxed manner and let the chest sink down to its original position.

6. Keep the hands and the knees apart and the head relaxed. Lift the right arm and stretch it perpendicular to the body and breathe in. Bring the arm back to the original position and breathe out. Repeat with the left arm and legs, one by one.

Repeat the above exercise, stretching one arm and the opposite leg, simultaneously. After the exercise, lie either on the back, or on the side, for 5 minutes, completely relaxed. All these exercises may be done twice a day.

Toe-touching Exercise: Stand with back, shoulders and head touching the wall, with hands raised above the head and their backs touching the wall. Then slowly bend the body so that the hands touch the floor (knees may be bent, if necessary) while breathing out all the time; continue to breathe out while returning to the starting position. Breathe in, and repeat the exercise ten times.

Sit-ups Exercise: Lie on the back on a mat with the arms and hands stretched out along the floor behind the head. With out-stretched hands, raise the body slowly and start breathing out; continue to raise the body and breathing out until the fingers touch the toes (the knees may be bent, if necessary). Return to the original position while continuing to breathe out. Rest and breathe in before repeating. Do it ten times.

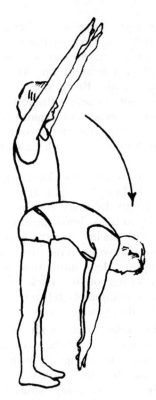

Toe-touching Exercise

Sit-ups Exercise

Exercise for Relief During an Attack

In a kneeling position with arms and head resting on a table or chair, breathe out slowly while gradually curving in the abdomen. Then let the abdomen relax and see the air enters the chest without any effort. Let the shoulders and chest relax. Do this slowly, otherwise it would cause wheezing.

The following are some of the important points to be particularly observed while doing exercises.

**Comfortable Sitting Possition
During Asthma Attack**

1. Clear the nose and breathe in through the nose, and breathe out through the mouth with a whistling or hissing sound.
2. When breathing in, keep the upper chest still, so that breathing in is performed by the diaphragm.
3. When breathing out, the whole chest should relax.
4. All exercises should be performed slowly without tiring the muscles.
5. The exercises may be repeated many times a day, so that the habit becomes second nature.

Expiration-Inspiration Ratio

The time taken for inspiration and expiration is very important for an asthma patient. Generally speaking, expiration should be longer than inspiration in the ratio of 3 : 2 approximately. This applies during both rest and exertion of any kind. Speed is relatively unimportant. The patient should try to fit this rhythm to the rate at which he is breathing. When he is breathless, he should breathe within his wheeze; any attempt to force expiration will only increase the wheeze and the spasm. He should do gentle, quick breathing with a longer expiration, while gradually reducing the speed.

Breathing exercises can be learnt by asthma patient within three to six weeks. If he likes, he can do them himself or learn from a physiotherapist.

Exercises for Children

The parents must be taught the techniques that the child should adopt when he has breathlessness. During an attack, the child can also perform the breathing exercises while lying down. Small children find it easy to sit on their heels and lean forward, their head and arms supported on a pillow; this makes lower chest breathing much easier.

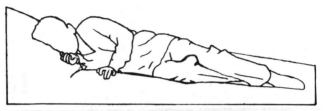

**Comfortable lying Position
During Asthma Attacl**

Children must be encouraged to play games, and to know that with exercise some breathlessness gets normal.

16

Yogic Exercises for Asthma

Though yoga is not primarily a method of treatment of diseases, one does find in later yogic literature, especially in the Hatha yoga texts, many passages indicating the curative and prophylactic values of different yogic practices. *Hatha-yoga-Pradipika* states that in all diseases, the skillful physician should carefully administer treatment according to the methods prescribed by the science of medicine and also administer yogic treatment. For a long time, utmost secrecy was maintained by yogis about these methods, in the fear and belief that they would lose their efficacy if made known to the uninitiated. The yogic texts do hold out such cautions.

During the past few decades, due to the efforts of a few educated enthusiastic students of yoga, the yogic practices have been used and investigated in the treatment of some of the diseases including asthma. Details about one such study conducted on asthma patients are available from Kaivalyadhama, Lonavla and are described below.

Padmasana

Techniques

The following procedure was adopted: among others, *Savasana* (Corpse pose) with *Pranadharana* and *Makarasana* (Crocodile pose) were taught to the patients.

Those having a history of chronic colds and sinusitis were taught *Neti-kriya* (nose cleaning) with water and a rubber catheter. *Neti-kriya* was also done with salt water, with diluted milk and with honey. When done with salt water, the procedure was to vary the salt content and temperature and ultimately to use only

Shavasana

ordinary water (slightly below body temperature and not too cold). This procedure is said to develop resistance in the nasal mucous membrane to withstand variations in temperature and the barometeric pressure of the environment. When *Neti* was done with diluted milk, the procedure was to add milk to water; the quantity of milk being increased gradually till a 50-50 water and milk solution was used. This was done with the intention of developing resistance against proteins. When *Neti* was done with honey, with gradually increased proportions of 1 : 25 per cent, this was

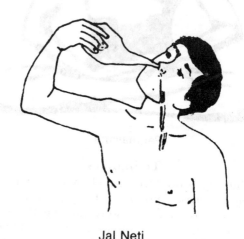

Jal Neti

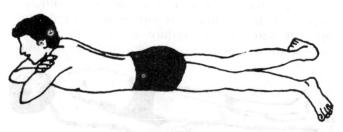

Makarasana

supposed to develop resistance against different pollen grains in the air.

Patients having cough with expectoration were taught *Dhautis* which included *Vaman-danda* (cleaning with a stick) and *Vastra Dhauti* (cleaning with a cloth). These helped in removing mucoid secretions from the stomach. *Vastra Dhauti* helped in the further removal of excessive mucous from the stomach.

For effective removal of sputum from the lungs, *Kapalabhati Kriya* (diaphragmatic breathing) was also advocated.

Sutra Neti

Results

The results obtained were as follows: of the 124 patients admitted, fourteen could not continue in this study as they were suffering from other diseases. Eighty-seven patients (76%) had no attack during the course of active treatment of two to four weeks and showed an all round improvement in both clinical and laboratory assessment. Twenty-three patients (20%)

had no attacks during the course of active treatment had no attacks during the course of active treatment but clinical and laboratory assessment did not show satisfactory improvements. Four patients (40%) had some mild attacks during the course of active treatment but clinical and laboratory assessment did show some significant improvement. All the patients showed some improvement as far as attacks were concerned in the clinical and laboratory assessment.

Conclusions

Those who have worked on the problem of asthma, have come to feel that *Dhautis*, especially, are very effective in averting an attack of asthma. Patients having a history of chronic colds, sinusitis, bronchitis, along with asthma, show good improvement in the follow up. The frequency and duration of the attack and the quantity of medicines needed to overcome the attack are definitely reduced in all the patients after this treatment.

Yogic procedures, as described already, help patients of asthma. They also help in reducing the dose of medicines needed, wherever they alone cannot bring about complete relief.

17

Psychological Factors in Asthma and their Management

Hippocrates, the Greek physician, as early as the fourth century B.C., noted the relationship between asthma and emotions and stated that "an asthmatic, if he were to master his own condition, must guard against his own anger."

The history of medical knowledge concerning the role of psychological factors in asthma, is a long one. Until allergic phenomenon was discovered, asthma was considered primarily a nervous disease, and was referred to as "Asthma nervosa" in older text-books of medicine.

The mechanism whereby the psychological factors cause asthma, however, remains obscure till today.

Personality Type of the Patient

A lot of work has been done on the personality type of the asthmatics. Dr. Bastiaans and Dr. Groen in 1955, described the following characteristics in the personality of the asthmatics.*

1. Marked egocentricity.
2. A tendency towards domineering behaviour.
3. A tendency towards impatient and impulsive behaviour.
4. A diminished capacity for adaptation to unfavourable life situations.
5. A marked emotional hypersensitivity.
6. A marked need for love and affection.
7. Stubbornness, often of an infantile type.
8. Strong reactions of jealousy and rivalry.
9. Lack of communication with others.

S.B. Singh and his colleagues in 1977, in India, studied personality traits in asthmatic children and found the following traits with greater consistency:

1. Over-anxiety.
2. Lack of self-confidence.
3. Deep-seated dependency.
4. High incidence of behaviour problems.

Parental Attitudes

The importance of parental attitudes in child asthmatics has been stressed by many researchers. Unsatisfactory parental attitude, especially of the mother, is found to be important in the causation and precipitation of attacks of asthma. Studies on parental attitudes have indicated a range of attitudes from rejection to over-protection.

Dr. Abramson, in 1954, clarified that the disturbance in the parent-child relationship was not parental rejection but rather "engulfments" of the child by the

---

*Reader please bear with the psychiatric terminology. Even though some words may be difficult, yet, I am sure, you can understand their meanings. If I were to explain their exact connotations, they would occupy more space than this chapter does, and yet I may cause confusion.

wilful and over-solicitous mother so as to force the child to be dependent on her and to devolop in such way as to satisfy her needs.

A Recent Study

A study entitled "Relative roles of allergy, respiratory infections and psychological environments in cases of bronchial asthma in children" was conducted in 1979 at the V. Patel Chest Institute under the author's guidance. One hundred children were studied.

Fifty-two per cent of the cases were assessed to have fear and anxiety, 40 per cent dependence on the mother and 32 per cent strong superego. Some children showed more than one such traits. However, no specific personality type could be associated with the patients studied. It is quite possible that the above traits in children were the result of the disease rather than the cuase of it.

As regards the parental attitudes in these cases, 36 per cent showed a marked degree of anxiety, and 41 per cent showed tendencies. Mothers showed these traits more predominantly than the fathers. The high incidence of anxiety and neurosis in the mothers of both the long-and short-duration cases is, perhaps, indicative of the prevailing emotionally charged environment in the home. Such environments can lead to similar tendencies in their children, learned either directly or by identification with the mother.

In the above study, it was also found that in 10 per cent of the cases, increase in the number of asthmatic attacks occurred during the examination period.

Control of Tension in Asthmatics

Most of the studies conducted so far indicate that mental tension and asthma are interlinked in many ways. When the tendency to get asthma is present, an attack of asthma can occur when the patient is tense. Fear of the next attack can itself set in an attack. The more tense the person the severer the attack. So long as the person is under tension, it is difficult to get rid of the attack in spite of all types of medications. That is why in some very tense patients, a mild sedative is also given, besides other anti-asthma drugs. Care is taken however, that even this mild sedative does not unduly depress respiration.

An asthma patient who feels that he/she gets tense sooner than most others, should learn and practice to remain calm under different environments, as well as during an attack. Relaxation of the mind and the body both, are required. For the mind to be relaxed, a correct objective appraisal of the situation is necessary. If it is the fear of an attack of asthma, an adequate information as to how and why an attack of asthma occurs—as has been told all along in this book—should be very helpful. The very purpose of this book has been to do just that.

Let me also assure you that an attack of asthma can be prevented from occurring. Also an attack can be treated with the medicines that we have with us now. In fact, asthma is a much lesser evil than most other diseases, because in between the attacks most of the patients feel quite normal. In the process of living with asthma, the patients come to learn as to what to do in various situations of the disease, so that they need lesser and lesser help from their doctors. Many children do grow out of asthma, and in adult patients, ordinarily, there is no diminution in their life span.

In order to lessen tension in general, an asthmatic—like other persons—should take care about the following:

1. • Regular daily habits is a must.
2. Morning walk/exercise, simple well-balanced diet, regular hours of work and sleep should be observed.
3. Packing too much work or ambitions in 24 hours

of the day should be avoided so that there is no unnecessary hurry and worry.

4. A simple·prayer to God for all that he has given to us, or sitting relaxed in meditation or just relaxing lying down in *Shavasana* is very helpful for all of us living in modern urban environments.

More important than all other things is to *accept the situation*. It serves no purpose to think "why only I got asthma, while others have been spared?" Nobody in the world has all the capabilities and no liabilities. Everybody has some gifts from God, not all gifts. Think in terms of "the half-full cup rather than the half-empty cup".

And now about the people who are around an asthma patient. This applies particularly to parents of the asthmatic children. This book by telling the "how and why" of many questions with regard to asthma, should allay their worst fears. Asthma can be prevented; asthma can be treated and controlled, and many children grow out of asthma. As and when the child is in an attack, he needs proper medication. Frequent change from one physician to another does not help. There is no immediate cure of asthma, the way we have for malaria. The attack needs to be controlled and the future course of action understood properly.

A few days back, a well-to-do and well educated lady came to my clinic with her nine-year old male asthmatic child who was not in an attack of asthma, and asked "Doctor, will this child survive?" While I was annoyed with this question being put in front of the child, the child himself looked perplexed and aghast. Such type of loose thoughts and speech must be avoided. It makes everybody tense and the child gets terrified and lands into a vicious cycle of tension-attack-tension.

Remember, that an asthmatic patient needs only a little more care, but no demonstration of sympathy or anxiety.

18

Asthma in Children

Asthma, many a time, starts in childhood, but the
picture of asthma then is different from that
observed in adulthood. In children, generally speaking,
asthma is present as recurrent attacks of cough and
wheezing only; in some attacks, it is accompanied by
fever and breathlessness also. Breathlessness in asthmatic children, usually, does not come in the form of
paroxysmal attack.

This picture of asthma has to be recognized clearly,
otherwise in the time lost in making a correct diagnosis
there is always the danger of chest deformities developing in the pliable bony cage of the children.

Premonitory Symptoms

Children who have other allergic symptoms are more
liable to get asthma. These symptoms are:

a) Unusual and persistent colic;
b) Need for frequent changes of feeding formulas;
c) Unexplained diarrhoea or constipation;

d) Extreme likes and dislikes for certain foods;
e) Excessive vomiting;
f) Unexplained skin rashes;
g) Discharge of pus from the ears (otitis media).
h) If one or both the parents have some allergic disorder, there is a likelihood that some of their children may also have it, may be in the form of asthma.

Treatment

Usual bronchodilator drugs, as given in adults, are useful in children as well. Only that they have to be given in reduced dosage, according to the age and weight of the child. For children, these drugs come in the form of liquids, or syrups and the easily accepted. Tedral liquid, if necessary, with a liquid preparation of salbutamol are usually adequate in mild cases.

Corticosteroids are only rarely needed if all other measures are taken adequately. But, in case an attack of asthma does not subside in spite of all the other measures already undertaken, there is a need for giving cortisone for a few days, in order to bring the child out of the attack; cortisone can then be tapered of in a few days time.

It is not advisable to give antibiotics to children unless there is clear evidence of infection. Unnecessary administration of antibiotics like tetracyclines are liable to colour the teeth permanently. Even though milk teeth fall out, the permanent ones that have still to come are already being formed and can become discoloured; this has particularly a damaging effect in the case of girls. Penicillin is more liable to cause reactions in allergic children than in other people, hence antibiotics in asthmatic children should only be given when there is clear evidence of a bacterial infection.

Finding out to what the child is allergic and

subsequent hyposensitization, if the allergen cannot be eliminated from the diet, is sometimes resorted to. However, it is difficult to get cooperation from the children. Hence, if other measures give relief, skin testing and hyposensitization may be held in abeyance for the time being.

Preventive Measures Against Asthma

Parents who have some symptoms of allergy are more likely to have children with allergy. Hence they require to take special precautions in the case of their children.

It has been reported that a breast-fed infant has one-seventh the chance of getting allergic eczema than the bottle-fed baby. An early introduction of solid foods in the diet of an infant also predisposes him to allergy.

Milk should be boiled before giving. Eggs should not be introduced in the diet before six months of age and after that boiled eggs should be given; *unboiled egg should never be given.* The introduction of foods that are most commonly allergenic. i.e., egg, wheat, fish, cocoa, etc., should be delayed.

Dust-Free Environments: The environments of a child who is potentially allergic, are very important. The child's bed-room should be best reserved as a place for sleeping, not for play. It should be kept as free as possible of inhaleable allergens. The furniture should be of a type which does not promote the presence of dust or mould spores. The mattress may be enclosed completely in a tight dust-proof casing, or a foam rubber mattress may be used. Dust-collecting drapes, bedspreads and wool rugs should be avoided. Blankets should preferably be made of synthetic fibres and covered with a cotton case. The child's bed should not be situated next to an open window since a chill caused by cold weather may give rise to symptoms.

Pets should not be allowed in the bedroom and are best kept out of the house, otherwise dog or cat dander may become part of the house dust. Stuffed toys should be kept out of the crib.

House cleaning should, preferably, be done when the child is away at school. White-washing and painting, etc., should be done when the child is out of the house.

Protection from Infection: A potentially allergic child should be immunized like any other child, against whooping cough, diphtheria, tetanus, typhoid, cholera and polio. Because so many allergic children are sensitive or sensitizeable to eggs, vaccines containing egg protein are a special hazard to them and should be avoided. Where there is a doubt, a preliminary scratch test with the vaccine may be done, and only if no reaction is elicited, the vaccine should be given.

Every precaution must be taken to see that the child does not get a bacterial or viral infection, but if he does, he must be treated promptly and adequately. Many a time, symptoms of allergy are precipitated during such an infection.

Children predisposed to allergy are likely to do well in a dry climate, away from the seashore and, also, in a climate which is free of industrial air pollutants.

Special recommendations are some times offered for allergic pregnant mothers. Some doctors believe that strong allergenic foods such as eggs, milk, nuts and fish should be curtailed considerably during pregnancy; others take a modified position and allow the mother to have all foods but not in excessive amounts.

Does the Wheeze Always Mean Asthma?

A case of wheezing and breathlessness may or may not be a case of bronchial asthma. There are other diseases also in which wheezing and breathlessness are the main or subsidiary symptoms. These conditions need to be recognized properly.

It is necessary to differentiate asthma from acute

bronchiolitis, presence of a foreign body in the bronchial tree, pressure on the main bronchi from a tuberculous gland, enlarged thymus pressing upon the trachea, bronchiectasis, cystic fibrosis of the pancreas in which lung involvement is predominant, and congenital diseases of the heart.

When it is a foreign body in the respiratory tract causing wheeze and difficulty in breathing, the onset is sudden and there is usually a history of having inhaled a foreign material.

Without a proper and adequate investigation, a wheeze should not be invariably considered as asthma.

Post Natal Care For Your Newborns

Do's

- Preferably breast-feed your child. Chances of getting allergies is more in bottle-fed babies.

- Boil the milk properly before giving.

- Introduction of common allergenic foods such as eggs, wheat, fish, cocoa, etc. should be delayed.

- Dust proof casing or a foam rubber mattress should be used. Dust free environment is very important for a child.

- Keep the pets away from the baby's bed-room.

- Stuffed toys should be kept out of the crib.

Dont's

- Avoid early introduction of solid foods in the diet.

- Unboiled eggs should be avoided in diet before nine months of age and after that boiled eggs should be given.

- Dust collecting drapes, bedspreads, wool rugs and carpets should be avoided.

19

Enlarged Tonsils
and Asthma

Tonsils stand like two sentinels on either side of the pharynx, the middle portion of the throat. They They defend the body against germs or other dangerous substances that try to enter our body through the mouth or nose. They try. to trap these germs inside their structure and then with the help of lymphatic cells, of which the tonsils are made, produce protective antibodies. These antibodies circulate in the blood and fight those intruders which somehow manage to bypass the tonsils. The antibody forming tissue is present in the other parts of the body also, but in the shape of the tonsils, it forms the first line of defence of the body.

During childhood, the body is exposed to many germs for the first time, and needs to be protected against them. In this process of protecting the body, the tonsils work vigorously and in some children get unduly enlarged.

Whether the enlarged tonsils should be removed or not is a controversial question; still more controversial is whether the tonsils should be removed in a child who has some allergic manifestations such as cough and wheeze. There are three different views available on the subject:

1. That tonsils act initially as the site and subsequently as a source of infection in the body. Their removal would favourably influence the course of asthma or even prevent its occurrence in a susceptible individual.

2. That tonsils perform an important function in preventing the spread of infection from the nose and throat into the bronchi and the lungs. Their removal, therefore, would lead to a mild asthma developing into a severe one or might even precipitate asthma in a susceptible individual.

3. That the presence or the removal of tonsils makes no difference to the allergic state of an individual. The removal of tonsils can, therefore, neither prevent asthma nor precipitate its onset.

Allergic children are, no doubt, more susceptible to infections, particularly those of the throat and the chest. If evidence of infection in the throat exists and if the infection localised in the tonsils appears again and again, it may be that the tonsils need to be removed. But removal of the infected tonsils should be done with the understanding that it may have no effect upon the asthma which the child is suffering from. At best, the removal of an infected tonsils may do away with one factor which may, indirectly, have something to do with the aggravation or precipitation of asthma, but it does not touch the basic factor of allergy in the child. Until this is investigated and tackled properly, symptoms of asthma may continue to appear. A comparative study of asthmatic children whose tonsils had been removed and those in whom they were allowed to remain, showed no statistical difference in the severity of the symptoms of asthma; both groups showed the same percentage of mild, moderate and severe case of asthma.

Even those who advocate that surgical removal of the tonsils (tonsillectomy) in asthma patients proves useful, agree that the benefits derived from tonsillectomy are greater in he first post-operative year than in the second. If tonsils are the cause of trouble in asthma patients, one whould expect the improvement in symptoms to increase rather than decrease as time passes.

Thus we see that there is no difference in the indications for removal of the tonsils in asthmatic or non-asthmatic children and these indications are:

1. Chronic infection of the tonsils and adenoids.
2. Marked enlargement of tonsils and adenoids, causing interference in breathing and swallowing.
3. Recurrent ear infections.

An asthmatic child with merely enlarged tonsils needs to be investigated for allergy on the same lines as any other asthmatic patient. The cause of allergy, whether inhalant or ingestant, must be found out, and then either eliminated from the diet or submitted to proper hyposensitization, provided the child is cooperative.

20

Asthma in Older People

A sthma manifests itself differently in children, adults and elderly people. In children, it is usually manifested as cough and wheeze; in adults, as paroxysmal attacks of breathlessness; in older people, while paroxysmal attacks may continue, exertional dyspnoea (breathlessness on exertion) also set in due to the complications of chronic bronchitis and emphysema. While adult asthma patients feel normal in between the attacks, older patients continue getting breathlessness on exertion even while they do not have the asthma attack.

Those who first start getting asthma in their old age, fare far worse than those who have had the onset in their youth.

Treatment

Treatment of asthma in older patients needs much more attention and care. Male patients having enlarged prostate gland face a particular difficulty; administration of bronchodilators containing ephedrine may lead to hesitancy in passing urine or lead to the retention of urine.

Corticosteroids can lead to softening of bone (osteoporosis) and the fracture of already fragile bones. Some older patients who had been taking corticosteroids for a long time are known to have fractured their ribs on coughing. The incidence of tuberculosis is also appreciable in those who take corticosteroids; symptoms of such a condition may not become clear till much later.

Injection of adrenaline in status asthmaticus endangers the heart and blood vessels of those who have hypertensive heart disease.

In older people, it is not easy to differentiate whether it is certainly a case of asthma because cough and breathlessness in this age-group are symptoms of many other diseases also, some of which have been already mentioned in Chapter Two.

21

Seasonal Sneezing or Hay Fever

Bouts of sneezing occurring in a particular season, in medical terminology called *seasonal allergic rhinitis* and in layman's language *hay fever*, is the commonest form of allergy. Hay fever does not have any connection with hay. It is the seasonal occurrence of sneezing and running of the nose with congestion in the nose and itching in the eyes and nose. Year after year, these symptoms occur in a patient in the same seasons while in other months, he feels perfectly normal. It may occur in children or in older people, but, mostly it occurs among young people. Males and females are equally effected by it. The symptoms may be mild or very severe and distressing.

Hay fever occurs in those who have inherited an allergic background. As the pollens to which they are allergic appear in the air in a particular season of the year, the symptoms of the disease occur seasonally.

Symptoms
The onset of sneezing may be gradual or quite sudden, depending on the degree of exposure to the particular

pollens to which the patient is allergic. When the onset is gradual, the attack is usually preceded by a mild sensation of itching and burning of the eyes or mild irritation in the nose or itching of the palate inside the mouth. Attacks of sneezing start especially in the early hours of the morning when there is a sudden increase in the concentration of pollens in the air. Marked nasal congestion and profuse running of the nose and eyes follow the sneezing paroxysms.

As the attack progresses, the nasal mucous membrane becomes highly sensitive and responds with sneezing to small stimuli which were previously innocuous, such as the slightest draft, strong odours, or minute amounts of dust.

Many patients suffering from hay fever also complain of various constitutional symptoms, such as lassitude, loss of appetite, drowsiness, etc. Some of these symptoms may be due to the self-administration of antihistamine drugs.

Accompanying Asthma: In some patients, symptoms of bronchial asthma also appear. They may start at the onset of the disease, or appear later. In certain cases, along with the symptoms of hay fever, there is a cough only and no bronchial spasm. Symptoms of cough and asthma may continue even when attacks of sneezing cease.

Diagnosis of the condition is not difficult and is revealed by the case history.

In the treatment of such cases, it is important to find out the pollen or pollens to which the patient is allergic. This is done by means of skin tests with the extracts of the pollens. Scratch or intracutaneous tests giving positive reactions for the pollens coupled with a confirmation of the same through consultation of the pollen calendar, confirms the causative pollens.

Treatment: Hyposensitization with the incriminated pollens yields excellent results in this condition.

Role of Antihistamines

Symptomatic treatment with antihistamine tablets is very helpful; one has to try one or more kinds of antihistamines to find out which one suits a person particularly well.

The name antihistamine suggests that these drugs work by acting against and destroying histamine that is produced in allergic reactions. This, it does to a large extent but since in an allergic reaction, other substances besides histamine are released as well, it is understandable that antihistamines do not abolish all the symptoms of an allergic reaction.

Antihistamines have proved most useful in cases of hay fever. Given at the beginning of the attack, they are most effective; they lessen itching, sneezing and running of the nose. Long-acting antihistamines can also be tried in these cases.

Antihistamines come in different forms: tablets, capsules, injections such as Avil, Phenergan and as mixtures alone or in combination with other drugs such as Actifed and Sudafet.

However, antihistamines are no substitute for a proper detection of the allergens and subsequent hyposensitization.

Side Effects: Almost all antihistamines cause drowsiness. If one drug proves unsuitable in this regard, another can be tried. Giving antihistamines with tea, coffee, also help in lessening the feeling of drowsiness. The drowsiness caused by antihistamines, sometimes, prohibits their administration during the day time, for example, when the patient has to drive a vehicle or to do some such active work.

In rare cases, central nervous system stimulation may be a side reaction with some antihistamines, producing symptoms such as irritability, tension, insomnia, etc.

Antihistamines should be given only when needed, and not continuously as a routine.

Prevention of Sneezing Attacks

In order to prevent getting attacks of sneezing of hay fever, the following precautions are helpful:

1. Avoid needles outdoor activities in the particular season.
2. Avoid gardening or farming.
3. If possible, keep bedroom windows closed and use air-conditioner.

If hay fever is untreated and continues on, it can cause permanent damage to the nasal mucosa and sinuses in the form of chronic infection. Symptoms of hay fever lessen as the patient grows older.

22

Perennial Sneezing or Perennial Allergic Rhinitis

Some patients have sneezing and a running nose almost all the year round.

Symptoms

A majority of them complain of a blocked or stuffy nose and of post-nasal discharge as well. Many of them snore at night because of this condition, and develop the habit of breathing through the mouth. They experience discomfort in the ears as well due to a blocking of the ear tubes that open in the throat called eustachian tubes.

Children develop a peculiar mannerism of wiping their nose: they elevate the tip of the nose with the palm of the hand and wriggle the nose and mouth from side to side; this gives them a temporary relief from the symptoms. Constant rubbing of the nose sometimes leads to the development of a crease across the nose, called the 'allergic crease'. The mucous membrane of the paranasal sinuses may also be involved in the allergic process and infections, causing blockage of the opening of the sinuses and accumulation of the secretions; there may be associated fever. The middle ear may get infected repeatedly, causing flow of pus from the ears. Some of the patients develop cough and wheezing as well.

Exposure to cold wind, sunlight, dusts and fumes etc. precipitate the onset of symptoms or aggravate them. These symptoms occur more often in the early morning, but may last throughout the day and even the night.

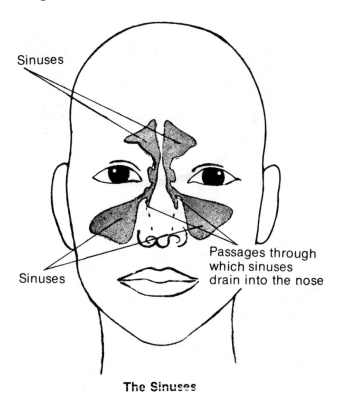

The Sinuses

Examination of the Nose

In the acute stage, examination of the nose, reveals a swollen, grayish-pale mucous membrane which is covered over with mucous secretion, the swollen mucous membrane may even be obstructing the nasal passages.

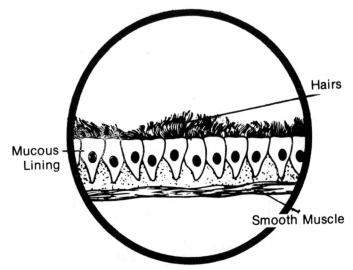

Hairs

Mucous Lining

Smooth Muscle

The Nose Lining

In the chronic stage of the disease, the nasal membrane may be swollen, baggy and pearl grey, with mucous and pus or even frank pus, if there is a superimposed infection. Nasal polyps in the form of bunch of grapes hanging from the mucous membrane may also be seen blocking nose.

Diagnosis

Diagnosis of the condition is helped by the history of the disease, a family history of allergy, and examination of the nose. Much more important, is the laboratory examination of the nasal secretions which shows a large number of eosinophil cell—a type of white blood cells which on staining take red colour, indicative of allergy.

But all this gives no indication of the agents to which the patient is allergic; this needs skin testing with the different allergens such as pollens, moulds and dust, etc.

Treatment

Exposure to some allergens, pollutants and irritants can be reduced. These include house dust, outside dust and dust that arises in different occupations. Strong fumes whether from the kitchen or the laboratory or strong perfumes should be avoided.

After the causative allergens have been found, hyposensitization is the best method of treatment. The results, however, are not as good as in seasonal sneezing or hay fever.

In the circumstances where arrangements for hyposensitization are not available or till such time as the effect of hyposensitization does not appear, drug treatment has to be given to provide relief from symptoms. Antihistamines help, but not as much as in seasonal cases. Nose drops containing ephedrine and antihistamines also give temporary relief; care must, however, be taken to limit their use to the minimum. Nose drops containing corticosteroids have not proved very helpful. Cauterization—burning the mucous membrane so as to make it insensitive—and such like measures which destroy viable (live) tissue do more harm than good. Nasal surgery is rarely, if ever, indicated.

Adequate improvement obtained after hyposensitization and drug treatment leads very often to disappearance of the nasal polyps as well; they need no surgical excision, unless they are obstructing the nose to the extent that respiration becomes difficult.

Differentiation from Common Cold

Frequent occurrences of the common cold, a virus infection, with super-added bacterial infection, sometimes makes it difficult to differentiate between it and the perennial allergic rhinitis. Common cold usually begins with malaise, aches and pains, diminished appetite and a slight rise of temperature. Running nose and sneezing occur either simultaneously or soon after. The nasal discharge is at first watery, but later it becomes thick. With the nasal obstruction, there may be headache, loss of sense of taste accompanied by mouth-breathing. The symptoms may persist for some days or even weeks.

History of the disease, family history, examination of the nose and nasal smear help to differentiate between perennial allergic rhinitis and common cold. A nasal smear does not show eosinophils in a viral infection, while it does so in a case of perennial allergic rhinitis. Presence of positive or negative skin tests against various allergens also help in differentiating the conditions.

23

Urticaria

Urticaria is one of the commonest manifestations of allergy, a majority of the people having it at one time or another. In most of these cases, it is a transient phenomenon occurring only once or twice. In some, it comes up only in a particular season; in others, it persists for weeks, months and years, making life miserable.

Urticaria may be localized at some part of the body or spread all over the body. It may occur as only a few spots or it may be confluent. Raised reddish areas of different shapes and sizes appear which cause itching and last from a few minutes to a few hours without leaving behind any trace. Fresh urticarial patches may continue appearing while the older ones disappear.

Urticaria may also be accompanied by swelling of certain parts of the body such as lips, tongue, hands and feet; the condition is called angio-oedema.

The swelling and redness of the skin in cases of urticaria is due to the release of histamine in the tissues.

Causes

Some of the causes of urticaria are:

1. Physical agents such as cold, heat, sunlight and mechanical pressure.
2. Emotional causes such as laughter, anxiety and panic.
3. Food articles such as nuts, seeds, fish, chicken, eggs, citrus fruits.
4. Drugs, out of which aspirin is the common offender; others are antibiotics, laxatives etc.
5. Sometimes insect bites and stings apart from causing local reactions of swelling.
6. Unknown causes, which form the majority of the cases.

Other Causes

Cold: Cold weather, cold winds, bathing with cold water, holding cold drinks in the hands or drinking them, are known to give rise to urticaria in susceptible people. Swelling of the mucous membrane of the mouth, difficulty in swallowing, pain in abdomen, or difficulty in breathing due to swelling of the glottis, are some of the other symptoms.

In order to make sure that the symptoms produced are a result of cold, it is necessary to perform a cold-immersion test. Immersion of the hand of a person allergic to cold in water at 5°C for five to ten minutes may be followed by a reddening and swelling of the hand. In some cases, symptoms such as blood flushing into the face, fall in blood pressure, and acceleration of the pulse may also appear. This may happen immediately or after a few minutes. The temperature level at which symptoms appear varies considerably.

Treatment consists, primarily, in the avoidance of exposure to cold. The use of antihistamines is helpful at times, but occasionally it is ineffective. Hyposensitization by exposing the hand or hands in water at progressively lower temperatures may be helpful. The hand is immersed in water at about 15°C for two to five minutes several times a day, and the temperature of the water is gradually reduced on successive days to about 6°C if the patient tolerates the lowered temperatures.

Heat: Heat, exertion or excitement can bring on urticaria in some cases. Hot baths, exposure to the heat of the sun, eating hot foods, sitting in a warm room, or strenuous exercise, can bring on an attack.

Diagnosis is made on the basis of the case history and confirmed by testing for heat exposure by having the patient put one leg in hot water. Attacks of generalized urticaria will be induced over the entire body except for the immersed leg which merely becomes flushed.

In general, treatment of **allergy to heat** is not satisfactory. In treating an acute reaction, any cooling agent such as cold water, cold air, or the application of alcohol to the skin will give some relief.

An attempt can be made to increase tolerance by exposing the subject gradually to higher temperatures, beginning by placing the hand in water at about 37°C and increasing the temperature to 43°C followed by a hot bath at 37°C.

Sunlight: In some rare cases, urticaria appears on exposure to sunlight. This is not due to heat, but to the sunlight itself. Characteristically, burning sensation is noted within 20 to 30 seconds after the exposure. This is followed by redness and a weal. The reaction may reach a peak in 10 minutes and persist for 1 to 2 hours.

In some cases, reactions occur only after photosensitizing agents have been ingested, such as sulphonamides, or applied to the skin, such as the tar derivatives contained in some cosmetic creams.

Diagnosis depends on the case history and the

reproduction of the lesions (injury, scar or wound) by exposure to sunlight. Treatment is generally unsatisfactory. Among the procedures that have been tried are a change of environment, wearing tinted glasses, staying indoors, avoiding known photosensitizing substances, coating the skin with agents capable of filtering out the injurious ray.

Mechanical Pressure

In some cases, a swelling of the skin (weal) can be produced if it is stroked with a nail. For demonstrative purposes, one can write a complete alphabet on the back of such patients by means of a nail. Swelling appears within ten minutes of the application of mechanical pressure. The condition is called *dermographism*. An injury to the skin in these cases produces marked swelling, sometimes accompanied by itching all over the body, and rarely with a dizzy feeling in the head.

There are many other causes of urticaria. Broadly, they may be classified as the taking of certain drugs and foods, the inhalation of certain pollens, coming in contact with some chemicals or fibres such as nylon and wool, parasitic infestations of the intestines, physical exertion and emotional stress and foci of infection.

The taking of certain drugs by sensitive individuals is a common cause of urticaria, and reactions due to them are on the increase. Penicillin, aspirin, laxatives, sedatives, hormones and vaccine injections are commonly incriminated. Penicillin either by injection, oral or as ointment is considered, by some, to be the commonest cause of urticaria now-a-days. It is, however, not easy to find out the causative drug, as urticarial lesions often appear days and weeks after the taking of the drug.

Among the foods that cause urticaria in sensitive individuals, are those eaten raw such as bananas, oranges, strawberries, groundnut, tomatoes and wheat; other suspected foods are eggs, chocolate, fish, lobster, oyster, and prawns.

Diagnosis

The causative factor in an individual case is found with difficulty and that too not very often. A thorough searching history of the patient is the most important single factor that helps in pin-pointing the cause. In chronic urticaria, the foods that a patient usually takes must be thoroughly checked, while in the case of a patient who gets isolated bouts of urticaria he must concentrate on foods that are eaten occasionally. Urticaria localized continuously or repeatedly at certain areas suggests the possibility of a contact with an allergenic substance. Pollens may be implicated when there is seasonal incidence.

Physical examination is important particularly with regard to the appearance and distribution of the lesions, the presence or absence of other skin lesions, and the evidence of an infection, or of associated or related diseases.

Skin tests in these patients with extracts of pollens, dusts, and foods commonly elicit some positive reactions, but their true significance can only be ascertained after correlating them with the case history and clinical trials. By themselves they carry no significance, so far as treatment is concerned, because many of these patients are known to have been, or later on, become allergic to other things as well. Skin tests with the drugs are unreliable and may prove dangerous as well.

Treatment

If an examination of the stool shows presence of a parasite, the proper treatment may in some cases be helpful. Foci of infection in the teeth, tonsils, and other places should be treated appropriately.

Commonly known allergic articles of diet such as eggs, fish, milk, chocolate, dried fruits, etc., should be eliminated and the results noted. If there is an improvement in the symptoms, then all the eliminated foods should be re-administered, one by one, and the effect of each noted. There should be an interval of at least one week before a new food is added to the diet. Patients should be warned against taking any pain-relieving tablets, laxatives, sedatives, etc.

As for symptomatic relief, various antihistamine tablets are available. The particular brand which will suit an individual can only be found by trial and error. As general measures:

1. Avoid excessive physical and mental stress.
2. Reduce or avoid physical irritation of the skin.
3. Avoid self-medication and consult your doctor.
4. Avoid histamine-releasing foods such as bananas, strawberries.

24

Allergic Eczema

Allergic eczema appears in individuals who have a family history of allergy. Besides eczema they may be, having one or other manifestations of allergy such as asthma or seasonal sneezing.

Symptoms

In children, it begins in the first year o life. The skin mostly over the cheeks, scalp and at the creases of the body is dry and cracked. Because of itching and irritation, it is red and sometimes oozing.

Initial lesions consist of dryness and redness over the skin with uniform pin-head size eruptions. There is an oozing of serum from these lesions. Crusts form over the oozing vesicles (minute raised lesions with fluid in them) and the whole area gets infected with bacteria, producing pus. At this stage, the child not only has irritation locally, but may also have a general reaction in the body in the form of fever.

If the eruption becomes chronic or is aggravated

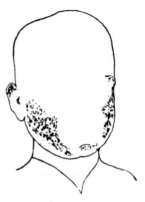

Infantile Eczema

by continued rubbing and scratching, swelling and thickening of the skin may result. Chronic lesion darkens the colour of the skin as well.

Causes

Causes of allergic eczema may be susceptibility to certain foods, pollens and dusts or to certain substances with which the skin comes in contact. Foods are more significant in infants and children, and inhalant allergens in adults. Wool and nylon clothes are also known to aggravate the lesions in some cases.

Among factors which often have an unfavourable influence on the course of the disease, are rapid changes in temperature, emotional tensions, dusty environments, alkaline cleansing agents, including common toilet soaps, contact with wool, greasy topical medicaments, and infections like cold, sinusitis. Disease associated with high fever, however, often exert a temporary beneficial action.

Diagnosis

Diagnosis of the offending allergens in these cases is very important in order to cure the condition. This is done by means of clinical tests of avoidance and re-exposure to the suspected items.

Skin tests are not very reliable indicators of the allergenic agents.

Treatment

Keeping the skin moist through application of creams, oils, ointments is helpful. Antihistaminic creams also reduce itching and thus lead to natural healing of the lesions. In severe cases, application of ointments containing corticosteroids proves helpful.

Some of the commonly used **substances** that cause this reaction and the **site of reaction** are as follows:

Substance	Site
Stockings, shoes, *chappals*	Feet
Clothing	Legs and body
Plants, vegetables, detergents, kerosene oil	Hands
Deodorant	Armpits
Necklace	Neck
Lipstick	Lips
Nose drops	Nose and area around the nose
Spectacles	Bridge of the nose
Cosmetics, razor	Face
Ear lobes	Ear-rings
Eye cosmetics	Eye lids and area around the eyes
Hair dyes	Forehead, behind the ears and back of the neck, scalp.

25

Contact Dermatitis

Contact dermatitis is the reaction in the skin caused by contact with a substance to which it has become allergic because of an earlier contact.

For the occurrence of contact dermatitis an allergic background in the persons is not necessary. Prolonged and recurrent contact is necessary to initiate this reaction. Any substance in sufficient amounts can cause this reaction. However, some substances are more likely to cause it than others.

Instances of contact dermatitis produced as a result of contact with certain substances, are not uncommon. A few years ago when rubber *chappals* with V-shaped straps first came in the market, hundreds of cases were reported of V-shaped lesions on the upper surface of the feet. Investigations revealed that there were some chemicals in the rubber to which the skin of the feet became allergic, and this led to the skin lesions.

Some hair dyes are particularly known to cause allergic reactions of the skin; oils and soaps cause allergic lesions of the skin. Chemicals, like sulphonamides, and antibiotics, like penicillin, also cause such lesions when applied in powder form or as an ointment. Some plants or plant products are notorious in this regard; these include marking-nut, henna, ak (Calotropis gigantea), *zaminkand, babchi,* mango, etc.

Contact dermatitis cases are on the increase as more and more people are exposed to newer and larger number of drugs and chemicals. It occurs in all age groups, more so in adults and older people, as they have been exposed to a larger number of substances to which they may become allergic.

The substances that cause contact dermatitis either produce irritation of the skin because of their inherent chemical nature or, are non-irritating in themselves and yet cause allergic lesions. The more concentrated a substance, the more readily it excites an allergic response. The liability of a person to become sensitive to the substances mentioned above varies from person to person.

Symptoms

The time interval between the first contact with the substance and for sensitization of the skin to develop symptoms, varies from one to three weeks. Once sensitization has developed, a subsequent contact leads to the appearance of the skin lesion within hours. The first symptom that a patient experiences is itching, which is usually localized to the area of contact, though it may spread to adjacent areas as well. The itching, at times, is very severe, which causes the patient to scratch, thereby hastening the skin reaction that is to follow. A redness is first noted in the affected area, which rapidly progresses to the stage of minute raised lesions with fluid in them (papules and vesicles).

In the chronic stage, there is confluence of lesions, leading to thickening of the skin, bacterial infection and pus formation. In the early stage of the disease there is almost always a line of demarcation between normal and abnormal skin. As time passes, the disease may spread to adjacent areas, and a localization pattern may no longer be evident. Even contact of the oozing secretions with other areas produces lesions, as the whole skin has been sensitized.

The severity and course of the disease depend on the sensitization potential of the patient's skin and the amount of contact. The lesions may be self-limited and not progress beyond the stage of itching, redness, and vesiculation. At other times, they may become chronic and continue on to the subacute and chronic stages of the disease.

The parts of the body most often affected are the exposed areas. The region or part of the skin involved, assists in determining the etiologic factor; leathers, fabrics, and dyes usually involve the feet, lower extremities and trunk; cosmetics cause reactions on

Marking Nut

the ·face and axillae (arm pit); toys cause lesions on the hands and upper extremities. Allergy to a particular metal such as nickel appears wherever articles made of the metal come in contact with the skin.

Allergy to Parthenium

Parthenium is a weed native to South and Central America. It was accidently introduced in India in 1956 as a contaminant with the imported wheat grain PL 480 scheme. The weed was first detected in Poona region, and now it grows in almost all parts of the country. It is abundantly growing in Maharastra, Karnataka, Andhra Pradesh, Uttar Pradesh, West Bengal, Jammu and Kashmir and Delhi. The weed is aggressive and can grow in any type of soil without any care. It is commonly known as, *gajar ghas*, 'carrot weed', or *chetak chandani*. Each plant reproduces profusely; the weed can complete 4 life cycles in a span of one year.

Clinical Picture

The initial *symptoms* are itching around sides of the neck and face. Slowly the itching spreads from face to 'V' of the neck, elbows, knees and may engulf the whole body. The itching produces swelling of the skin and watery discharge oozes out. Gradually the skin becomes thick, dark and lustreless. Numerous scratch marks can be seen. The continued itching makes the life of the patient miserable. Children and teenagers are, however less affected.

It is interesting to note that the weed in its native country is not very offensive.

All parts of the Parthenium have been chemically analysed and various chemical fractions isolated and structurally defined. Out of various chemical fractions Parthenin appears to be the chief culprit. This is abundantly found in leaves and fine hair present on the stem. The cause and effect relationship is proved by patch test, using either the crude plant parts or the antigenic extracts prepared from plant parts.

Treatment

Avoiding contact with the plant, either directly or indirectly, is considered the best treatment for patients suffering from Parthenium allergy. The conventional treatment with anti-allergy drugs and even more potent corticosteroids hardly makes any dent on the course of allergy. On the contrary, increased doses of cortisone cause various side effects.

Sun light does not cause the disease as such but existing disease is made worse. Therefore, to protect the patient from sun light is helpful as an adjunct to the treatment.

Prevention

It has been observed that if the patient is removed from the area infested with Pathenium weed, he remains well even without medication. Direct contact with the plant and indirect contact with the hair and pollen of the weed should be avoided.

By its invasion on agricultural land, several crops get infected with this weed leading to loss of yield. Realising numerous harmful effects, efforts are being made at various levels to check the growth of this noxious weed by the use of weedicides and biological control methods.

Allergy to Vegetable Products

Dermatitis produced as a result of contact with plant products is not uncommon, and each plant product has its own characteristic features. The black juice of the marking-nut *(Semecarpus anacardium)* produces vesicles on the skin; the fluid of the vesicle, when it comes in contact with other parts of the body, produces vesicles there as well.

The juice of marking-nut known as *bhilawa*, is used by washermen to put an identity mark on laundry clothes. These marks are usually made on the inside surface of the backs of collars, brassiers, vests and underwears. Dermatitis caused by it is seen on the part of the body where the marking comes in contact with the skin. A number of cases with such dermatitis have been seen in foreigners in India; local residents, it seems, are not very sensitive to it.

Application of *henna (Lawsonia inermis)* also leads to sensitization in some cases. This is usually in the form of minute skin eruption and causes oozing from the palms and soles, where *henna* is commonly applied for cosmetic or ritual purposes. Occasionally, due to contact with *henna* powder, dermatitis may occur over the whole face and other exposed parts of the body.

The latex which oozes out of *ak (Calotropis gigantea)* is strong irritant to the skin and mucous membranes

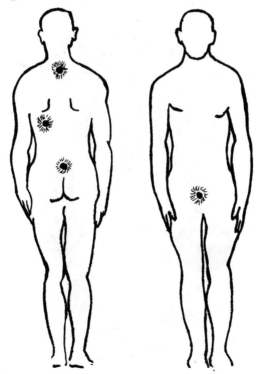

Common Sites of Marking Nut Dermatitis

which is used by some people to treat some skin diseases. When so used, it may be responsible for severe dermatitis in the form of eruptions, bullae or even ulcers.

The mango plant and the juice of its fruit are also known to produce allergic lesion of the skin. Contact dermatitis sometimes apperas in the form of eruptions on the limbs of children who climb mango trees. The first few drops that ooze out at the junction of the fruit and its stem, cause more severe reactions. The juice of the unripe fruit also gives rise to a high incidence of allergy and so does its peel. Mango juice when drunk does not usually cause dermatitis. Mango dermatitis is more common among foreigners, particu-

Elephant's Foot *(Zaminkund)*

larly those from the white races, than among the local population.

A vegetable called *zaminkand (Amorphophallus campanulatus)* is also frequenty the cause of sensitization. The juice of the tubers is irritant and cause itching, rednerss and urticaria in housewives handling this vegetable. This can be prevented by the application of vegetable oil on the hands before handling.

The seeds of *babchi (Psoralea corylifolia)* yield an essential oil which is used in the treatment of leucoderma, the white patches that develop on the skin of some persons. Contact with them can cause dermatitis and photosensitivity. In sensitive individuals, redness and blisters develop within a few hours of local application and these may be precipitated by exposure to the sun. This condition is frequently seen in skin clinics in India because *babchi* is used extensively by *vaids* and *hakims* in treating leucoderma.

Allergy to Cosmetics

A person may have been using the same cosmetic or hair dye, and yet become allergic to it after years of use. Hair dye is the worst offender in this regard. The rash from hair-dye allergy appears typiocally behind the ears, almost a day after application of the dye.

It is absolutely essential that a particular hair dye is tested on the forearms or behind the ears and observed for 24 hours, and if no rash is seen, only then it be used. If a hair dye is causing a reaction, its use must be stopped.

Allergy to Metals

The commonest offenders in this category are nickel and chromium and these elements are present in almost every metal that one comes in contact with daily, more so the ladies. These are present in jewellery, hair pins, hair rollers, razors, watch chain, zipper, belt buckle, clip, scissors etc. Chromium salts are present in leather and even in matchsticks. The treatment is avoidance of contact with the offender.

Allergy to Clothing

Skin allergy to clothing is not due to the fabric but to the variety of chemicals that it contains, particularly when it is new. Chemicals are contained in the dyes, the sizing material, finishing agents and the substances that make a cloth crease-proof. Reaction to clothing occurs where it is very tightly held against the skin or in the folds of the body.

In order to prevent or minimize allergy to clothing:

1. Never wear an unwashed garment.
2. When garments arrive from the washerman or dry-cleaner, air them in the open before use.
3. Use white cotton next to the body, wherever possible.

Diagnosis

Contact dermatitis is diagnosed from the history of the case, area distribution of the lesion and nature of the lesions. This may be confirmed by patch testing.

Patch Testing: This is to confirm the causative agent. By this, is produced on the patient's skin, a small lesion with the incriminating substance. The reliability of patch test depends on several factors; the most important of which is the material applied to the skin be non-irritant. If the test substances is known to be an irritant, only a very dilute solution of it should be used for testing so that no inflammation is produced.

The material to be tested, in appropriate dilution, is applied to the gauze part of an ordinary band-aid plastic patch. Ointments, creams and salves for testing are placed on the gauze part of the plastic patch before testing. If it be a fabric, small shreds moistened with distilled water are applied. If the material is solid or particulate fine shavings, filings or powders are placed on the moistened gauze. The patch is applied on the uninvolved, non-hairy portions of the skin, preferably on the arms, thigh, front or back of the body. The skin area is thoroughly cleansed and defatted with alcohol and ether, prior to application of the patch. To make sure that the patch remains in its proper position and does not loosen and come in contact with the surrounding skin, additional strips of adhesive tape may be applied along the edges. When the test patch is on, the patient should not take a bath or sit under a shower and should see that the test patch does not get dislodged accidentally. The patient should be alerted to remove the patch if severe itching, burning or pain is noted. The patches are generally removed, carefully, after 24 to 48 hours. A diagnostic reading is best done 24 hours after the removal of the patch.

Significant positive reaction to patch-testing establishes the patient's sensitivity to the test material. A negative result, on the other hand, does not necessarily exclude the material tested as non-allergenic in the patient.

Treatment

Success in treating dermatitis depends chiefly on the recognition and elimination of the cause, and once this has been determined, it should immediately be removed. Factors which aggravate certain contact reactions, such as mechanical, chemical and heat irritation, should also be eliminated. In case the patient cannot be taken away from the offending material, protective barriers such as gloves, socks, masks etc., may be tried, as they, sometimes, do prove to be adequate.

For treating an acute case of contact dermatitis, the affected part should be washed with soap and water, cleaned with alcohol and the vesicles ruptured. Then wet compresser soaked in a 10 per cent solution of tannic acid should be applied for 30 minutes. A calamine lotion or hydrocortisone lotion or cream should then be used. Antihistamines and corticosteroids given orally, prove useful in severe cases.

Prognosis

Contact dermatitis usually is an acute problem and tends to become chronic, unless the offending substance is detected and eliminated. It spreads by transfer to other parts of the body producing similar lesions over there. The best treatment is to detect and remove the offending substance from the patient's environment.

26

Allergy to Drugs

There has been a real increase in the number of drug allergy cases, essentially because of the increased use of a variety of drugs.

All drugs produced some reaction in the body. There are, however, some reactions which are produced only in certain people and not all of these latter reactions are allergic in nature. Such unexpected reactions may be due to any of the folowing causes: 1) overdosage 2) drug interactions, for example a prescription containing a tranquiliser and an antihistamine may cause excessive drowsiness 3) idiosyncracy, as for example, an asthmatic may get palpitation of the heart even if he takes 1/4 gm of ephedrine 4) side effects, as are observed in the form of drowsiness after taking antihistamines 5) secondary effects, such as, hesitancy in passing urine, or even retention of urine, on taking ephedrine, that occurs in older people due to an already enlarged prostate; and 6) allergic reactions. When a reaction occurs after administration of a drug, it is necessary to know its true nature.

Symptoms of an Allergic Reaction

The first time administration of a drug may cause no adverse reaction but its repetition a few days or weeks later may cause one. Reaction may occur due to a) administration, b) external application, or c) a person sensitized by external contact may suffer a reaction by later ingestion of the sensitizing substance or a related chemical.

Skin Lesions: The most common drug reaction is urticaria; others are fever, skin rashes, jaundice and hepatitis. The most severe reaction is of anaphylaxis. Asthma may also be caused.

Urticaria is caused by allergy to various drugs such as penicillin, streptomycin, aspirin, sulphonamides, barbiturates, insulin, liver extract and others. Skin tests are of little use in the diagnosis of drug for urticaria; the best course being to stop all medication and note the subsequent effects. Contact dermatitis due to drugs allergy has already been described. It may be produced by sulphonamides, antibiotics, local anaesthetics, antihistaminic drugs, and many other drugs that are applied on the skin.

Fever: Drug fever is a common complication of treatment with sulphonamides, thiouracil, para-aminosalicylic acid (PAS), arsenicals, and anticonvulsants. The onset typically occurs a week or more after the first use of the drug. The fever may reach upto 40°C and may be continuous or intermittent. When the offending drug is discontinued, the fever subsides as soon as it has been eliminated from the body, usually in a few days.

Drug fever may be accompanied by a skin rash The diagnosis may be suspected if unexplained fever develops during the administration of any of the commonly causative drugs and subsides when they are discontinued.

Some drugs which take longer to be eliminated, produce reactions which cause widespread lesions in the body, such as inflammation of the arteries, heart, liver, spleen, kidneys and lymph glands; the continued use of such drugs can lead to fatal consequences.

Blood Destruction: Destruction of the blood cells may occur as a result of allergic drug reaction. This may result from the use of aminopyrine, arsenicals, thiouracil, sulphonamides, gold and anticonvulsive drugs. Except for gold and arsenic, these drugs are rather quickly eliminated from the body and the tendency is to recover within a week of the drug being discontinued.

Allergy to Aspirin

The commonly used and innocuous looking aspirin is one of the regular offenders as far as allergic drug reactions are concerned. While most people who take the usual dose of aspirin suffer no immediate ill effects, there are some who are allergic to it and they suffer from a variety of adverse reactions. Skin rashes or urticaria over the whole body or over the eyelid, lips and face are known to occur after taking aspirin. Swelling of the tongue, throat and larynx is sometimes so severe that it leads to suffocation.

Much more serious, however, is the onset of asthma in susceptible persons, after repeated doses of aspirin. Upto 20 per cent of severely ill, adult asthma patients have been found to have aspirin allergy. Some of these patients are unaware of this until an asthma attack is experimentally provoked in them by giving them test doses of aspirin. Some of the characteristic features of asthma due to aspirin allergy are—persons with aspirin allergy may develop asthma upto three hours after taking the drug; because of this latent period, many patients fail to connect the taking of aspirin with the subsequent attack. Even after the patient stops taking aspirin, the asthma attacks usually continue. This occurs more frequently in adults than in children. Many patients have nasal polyps. Several asthma patients allergic to aspirin, show positive skin reactions to other allergens as well such as, pollens and dusts.

Skin tests with aspirin are generally negative; it is only the case history or the experimental trial that helps in the diagnosis of allergy to aspirin.

These patients must be warned of the presence of aspirin in many of the pain-killing and fever-relieving tablets and mixtures.

Allergy to Vaccines

Various vaccines cause allergic reactions in sensitive people. They also cause some non-allergic reactions and it is essential that a proper differentiation be made between them. Non-allergic reactions include local inflammatory reactions and systemic reactions such as fever, malaise, nausea and vomiting. Allergic reactions may pertain to the skin, the respiratory system, the nervous system, or the reactions may be anaphylactic in nature. The whooping cough vaccine or the triple vaccine can occasionally cause purpuric rash, fever or shock. Tetanus toxoid has been known to cause urticaria, joint pains or even anaphylactic shock. Virus vaccines, such as for influenza, in which the virus is grown in a chicken's embryo, give allergic reactions in patients sensitive to eggs. Antirabic vaccine, in which the virus has been grown on the neurological tissue, is known to cause neurological reactions in some individuals. Urticarial rash and increasingly severe local reactions at the injected sites provides indications of impending reaction.

The patient allergic to aspirin which, chemically, is acetylsalicylic acid, is also sensitive to foods which naturally contain salicylates. There are apricots, berries, currents, grapes, peaches, plums, tomatoes, cucumbers. These foods should be avoided by those who are allergic to aspirin.

Diagnosis

The single and most important factor in the diagnosis of a drug reaction is the awareness of the doctor, that the symptoms may be due to allergic drug reaction. Discontinuation of the drug leading to a cessation of symptoms confirms the diagnosis. Some drugs take longer to be eliminated from the body, hence the symptoms of a drug's reaction may continue for a few days after its cessation. Skin tests with drugs are not a reliable guide, and sometimes prove dangerous as well.

Precautions

Symptoms such as fever, general malaise, restlessness or drowsiness, nausea, headache, transient numbness, generalized rashes, oedema, or unusual respiratory symptoms, especially coughing or wheezing are warning symptoms.

Vaccines made of egg as medium, or serum injections made from non-human sources, for example, horses, must be given with care, and should be avoided where allergic reactions to them have been noted before. If tetanus toxoid immunization has been given within five years, do not give ATS, but give a booster dose of 0.5 ml of tetanus toxoid.

The amount and the duration of drug dosage are important. Repeated intermittent administration is more hazardous than continuous. The route of administration often effects the sensitizing index of the drug. The oral method is least likely to cause sensitization, the injections next, and an application to the skin or mucous membranes the most likely.

Individuals with a family or personal history of allergy, show a greater tendency to develop drug allergies than non-allergic persons; this is particularly true of the immediate reaction. Children are less allergic to drugs than adults. Drug sensitized individuals are much more likely to acquire new drug allergies than those without previous sensitization.

It is always safe to skin test the patient before giving an injection of an antibiotic, vaccine or toxoid. Inject 0.01 ml to 0.02 ml of 1:100 dilution of the drug intradermally into the forearm with a tuberculin syringe (for small, just visible weal). This is read in fifteen minutes. Positive reaction consists of swelling (weal), redness and itching. A control test with the same amount of saline solution on a corresponding area of the other arm at the same time, is also done.

Remember that a negative skin test is not a surety against the occurrence of an allergic drug reaction. If it is positive, the drug is certainly not to be administered.

While giving an injection, avoid the possibility of intravenous innoculation by drawing back on the syringe piston prior to injection. If blood enters the syringe neck or barrel, withdraw the needle and select another site. Press the injected area following the innoculation in order to avoid leakage into any blood vessels which may have been punctured. Avoid deposition of vaccine in or near large nerve trunks.

Treatment

Since most of the manifestations of drug allergy tend to subside as the causative agent is excreted, the most important point in treatment is prompt discontinuation of the medication. For symptomatic treatment of drug allergies cortisone and allied drugs are the most effective.

Desensitization is only occasionally helpful. Antihistamine given along with a penicillin injection is a dangerous procedure; antihistamine decreases or prevails upon minor allergic reactions but cannot help severe anaphylactic reactions.

Anaphylactic Reaction

A case of anaphylaction shock within seconds, minutes after injection, is treated with:

1. A tourniquet above the site of injection.
2. Adrenaline 0.5 ml to 1 ml intramuscularly or intravenously, repeated as needed
3. Antihistamines, but not instead of adrenaline.
4. Artificial respiration and oxygen, if needed.

27

Allergy to Penicillin

A **Case Report:** K., 35 years, female, attended the clinic in 1959, with complaints of asthmatic breathlessness and fever for the last two days. She had been having asthma attacks for the past six years. Subcutaneous injection of adrenaline 1/3 ml. slowly provided her relief from breathlessness within half an hour.

Her blood examination showed a total white blood count of 23500 cells per cubic millimetre with 7 per cent eosinophils. After she had been adequately relieved of her breathlessness, about an hour after the first injection of adrenaline, she was given an injection of penicillin, 0.4 million units. Within a minute, she started gasping, and within three minutes she became blue (cyanosed) and her pulse became almost imperceptible and heart sounds inaudible.

She was at once given a subcutaneous injection of adrenaline 1/2 ml, coramine 2 ml and Avil 2 ml. She was put on oxygen and isoprenaline bronchodilator administered through intermittent positive pressure breathing. In about fifteen minutes she began to show signs of improvement and within two hours, was back to normal.

A month later, she again came to the clinic with an attack of asthma. She was given an injection of adrenaline, and immediately started gasping for breath. The reaction looked like an anaphylactic shock. This time she could be revived within half an hour. Later, it was revealed that the syringe from which she had received the injection of adrenaline, had previously been used for giving penicillin, and even though the syringe had been washed clean and boiled, the remnants of penicillin from the previous injection were enough to cause an anaphylactic reaction in this patient who was extremely sensitive to it.

Allergic reactions to penicillin are very common. They range from urticaria to anaphylaxis; the latter can cause death within minutes.

An anaphylactic reaction to penicillin, generally speaking, begins wihin seconds or a few minutes after taking it. The following sequence is typical: there is a peculiar taste in the mouth or a sensation in the tongue, and a strange tingling in the extremities. Seconds later, there is severe constriction of the chest, and a choking sensation or dyspnoea develops with increasing rapidity and cyanosis—bluish discoloration of the skin resulting from an increased amount of un-originated haemoglobin in blood—occurs simultaneously with symptoms of collapse. The whole reaction is sudden and terrifying. Only the alertness to the possible danger and instantaneous availability of the necessary injections and apparatus, can save the life of the patient.

Types of Reactions

Anaphylactic reaction to penicillin is the most dangerous and the most dramatic; there are others which are less dramatic but more common. These may be categorised as follows:

Delayed Reaction: This reaction is the most common one and it is thus called because of its incubation period, usually of 7 to 11 days; the minimum may be five days and the maximum perhaps about eight weeks. It is the response to initial sensitization and not to the previous exposure to penicillin. Urticaria is by far the most common symptom; others are joint pains, malaise and fever.

Accelerated and Immediate Reactions: These reactions are much less frequent and occur only in patients who have been sensitized by previous exposure to penicillin. The accelerated reactions appear in a few hours or in two to three days, and the immediate type occurs within seconds or minutes or upto two hours later. Clinically, these may be mild or more often severe there may be urticaria, breathlessness, anaphylaxis.

Hyperallergic Reactions: These are rare and include more intense and accelerated reactions with bullous eruptions—a thin walled air-filled space within the lung, arising congenitally or in emphysema.

Contact Dermatitis: This is not a rarity and follows the topical application of penicillin in the ointment form or even otherwise. The eruption may be acute, or chronic.

Indirect Reactions: Patients sensitive to penicillin are known to get reactions from it even from indirect sources. If a cow or a buffalow has been given a penicillin injection for some infection, the taking of its milk by a patient sensitive to penicillin is known to cause reactions. Some of the chronic reactions, such as urticaria may be perpetuated by penicillin through such indirect and often undetected sources.

Anaphylactic reaction to penicillin can occur not only after penicillin is given by injection, but also when it is administered orally in the form of a tablet, or instilled into the eye, ears or nose, or when applied on the skin as an ointment

Those with a significant occurrence of asthma in their families, and a similar personal history of either asthma or hay fever, usually have a higher incidence of penicillin reactions. Children show a lesser incidence of penicillin allergy than adults.

The commonest reaction to penicillin is appearance of rash over the body.

Skin Test With Penicillin

A positive skin test, observed at 15 minutes and most safely elicited by the scratch method, is a definite warning signal of potential anaphylaxis. When the case history suggests the possibility of anaphylaxis, the test is most safely carried out with graded dilutions beginning with 100 units per ml. and increasing to 50,000 units per ml. If the scratch test is negative, then intracutaneous tests may be carried out with dilutions of penicillin varying from 1000 to 50,000 units per ml. employing 0.2 ml. as is done in standard allergy testing to produce a just visible test weal.

The positive delayed skin test reaction, read like a tuberculin test (to know whether a person is infected with TB germs) after 24 to 48 hours, for redness and swelling in the skin occurs in those who have had a previous reaction to penicillin. This reaction is sometimes associated with urticaria or minute eruptions.

A careful note should be made of the fact that a *negative skin test is no guarantee against adverse reactions to penicillin.*

Prevention

Penicillin should not be used unless absoutely necessary. Before prescribing or injecting penicillin, a careful history should be taken as to *a)* the frequency

157

previous penicillin treatments as it is the repeated exposure to this antibiotic that is more likely to result in shock, *b)* any evidence of a previous allergic reaction to the antibiotic, *c)* personal history of allergy and especially of bronchial asthma, as it is among allergic persons that anaphylaxis and fatalities occur the most, *d)* skin test by scratch method must be done and if negative by intracutaneous method.

Paradoxically, however, most patients who get anaphylactic shock give no past history of previous penicillin allergy, whatsoever.

An injection is best given in the outer arm rather than in the buttock or deltoid so that, if need be, a tourniquet can be applied proximally to delay absorption.

Treatment

In anaphylaxis, adrenaline 0.5 to 1.0 ml., is administered subcutaneously. It works as the most effective antidote; in extreme urgency, it may be given intravenously. A tourniquet should, if possible, be applied proximal to the injection site to delay absorption. The patient is placed in a recumbent position and if necessary, oxygen may be given with a bronchodilator through intermittent positive pressure breathing. Injection of antihistamine and intravenous cortisone can be helpful.

Desensitization with penicillin is too hazardous in patients with a history of an immediate or anaphylactic reaction.

Those who are allergic to penicillin or its derivatives may also be allergic to related drugs like ampicillin and amoxycillin.

Adrenaline	1 ml. ampoules of 1:1000—five 30 ml. Vial of 1 : 1000.	
Aminophylline	Ampoules of aminophylline of 250 mg. each.	
Deriphylline	1 ml. ampoules for 1/m injection—5.	
Antihistamines	One 10 ml. vial of injectable Avil (50 mg/ml). Avil tabs 25 mg. each	— 10 tabs.
Steroids	Decadron 2 ml. vial	— 5 vials
	Betnalan tabs	— 50 tabs.
	Prednisolone tabs	— 50
Syringes	Tuberculin syringes	— 2
	2 ml all-glass syringes with needles.	— 2
Tourniquet		

TEST YOUR SELF

Is Your Cough Allergic in Nature?

		Yes	No
1.	Does the cough occur in a particalar season or change of season?	☐	☐
2.	Is the cough aggravated in particular season or change of season?	☐	☐
3.	Is it accompanied by bouts of sneezing as well?	☐	☐
4.	Is coughing more at night than during the day time?	☐	☐
5.	Did you have eczema in your childhood?	☐	☐
6.	Is there history of bouts of sneezing, eczema or coughing in the family, i.e., parents and siblings.	☐	☐

Interpretation

If the answer to even two of the above questions is in the affirmative, the cough is allergic in nature.

Is Your Child Allergic to a Food?

		Yes	No
1.	Does he get rash around his lips and inside the mouth after taking a particular food?	☐	☐
2.	Does he vomit a particular food each time he takes it?	☐	☐
3.	Does he get abdominal colic?	☐	☐
4.	Is he losing weight because he cannot retain a particular essential food, e.g., milk?	☐	☐
5.	Has he a reddish oozing rash on his face?	☐	☐

Interpretation

The more the "Yes" answers, the more the chances of allergy to an article of food.

Are the Child's Symptoms due to Asthma?

	Yes	No
1. Has he frequent cough?	☐	☐
2. Has he frequent running of the nose?	☐	☐
3. Does he get cough, sometimes followed by fever?	☐	☐
4. Has he a wheeze in his chest? This can be ascertained by putting your ear against his chest.	☐	☐
5. Has he or had he earlier oozing rash on his face?	☐	☐
6. Does he or did he get abdominal colic at any time?		

Interpretation
The more 'yes' he scores, the more likely he has asthma.

Weekly Self-Assessment Chart for the Asthmatic June 1, '88 to June 7, '88

Symptoms & Treatment			Sun.	Mon.	Tues.	Wed.	Thurs.	Fri.	Sat.
Symptoms									
1. Cough & Wheeze			+	+	+	+	+	+	+
2. Breathlessness			–	–	–	–	+	+	+
Treatment									
3. Tedral ⎤									
Salbutamol ⎬	No. of tabs.		–	–	–	+	+	+	+
Deriphylline ⎦									
4. Deriphylline ⎤	No. of injs.		–	–	–	–	–	–	–
Aminophylline ⎦									
5. Antibiotic Caps.			–	–	–	–	–	–	–
6. Corticosteroid tabs			–	–	–	–	–	–	–
Corticosteroid inj.			–	–	–	–	–	–	–

Scoring Method

Cough & Wheeze   Present (+) = 1 point,   Absent (–)
Breathlessness   Present (+) = 1 point,   Absent (–)

Tedral ⎤	No.	Taken (+) 6 tabs =	1 point,	Not taken (−)
Salbutamol ⎬	of	More than 6 tabs =	2 points,	
Deriphylline ⎦	tabs.			
Deriphylline ⎤	No.	Taken (+) inj =	2 points,	Not taken (−)
Aminophylline ⎦	of			
	injs			
Adrenaline		More than 1 inj =	3 points,	
Antibiotic Caps		Taken (+) =	1 point,	Not taken (−)
Corticosteroid tabs.		Taken (+) =	2 points,	Not taken (−)

Total Points

Assess the points you scored at the start of the treatment and then see whether points are decreasing or increasing. Accordingly, either reduce or increase the medicine with the advice of the doctor. Remember, if you score less points that means you are improving.

Is Your Skin Rash Allergic in Nature

		Yes	No
1.	Does the rash appear and disappear repeatedly?	☐	☐
2.	Is the rash raised from the skin?	☐	☐
3.	Does it cause itching when it is there?	☐	☐

4.	Has the rash any relation to:
	   a. heat,
	   b. cold,
	   c. exertion or
	   d. emotional state?
		☐	☐

5.	Does the rash appear after taking a particular food, e.g., chocolate, egg, fish.	☐	☐

Interpretation

'Yes' to any of the above questions indicates that the rash is allergic in nature.

Are You Allergic to Hair-Dye?

		Yes	No
1.	Does the need to scratch on the scalp occur after 24 hours of the application of the dye?	☐	☐
2.	Is there itching behind the ears and nape of the neck after 24 hours of the application?	☐	☐
3.	On examination, is there redness and raised spots on the scalp?	☐	☐

Interpretation
If the answer to any one question is 'Yes' you are allergic to that hair-dye, and stop using it.

Glossary

Adrenaline	A hormone secreted into the blood by adrenal gland present in the abdomen. Adrenaline injection removes spasm of the bronchi and is effective in anaphylactic reaction.
Allergen	A type of antigen which is harmless to most people, but in allergy-prone people causes asthma or sneezing when it is inhaled, eaten, given by injection, or when the person's skin comes in its contact.
Aminophylline	A type of drug which has the effect of dilating bronchi in cases of asthma.
Ampoule	A sealed glass tube, from which the liquid material is taken after breaking its head.
Anaphylactic reaction	A serious and acute allergic reaction in which there is severe spasm of the

	bronchi, difficulty in respiration, shock, and if untreated, may cause death.
Antibody	A substance produced in the body as a result of entrance of an antigen.
Antigen	A substance which can produce antibodies in the body, and react with them to cause antigen-antibody reaction.
Beta-2 stimulator drug	A new type of drug which causes drug dilation of the bronchi in an asthma patient without causing palpitation.
Bronchodilator	Which dilates the constricted bronchi as in the case of asthma.
Bronchitis	Inflammation of the bronchi. It is considered chronic when it has existed for over two years.
Bronchospasm	Construction of the bronchi.
Cardiac asthma	Symptoms more or less like asthma, but who primary cause is heart disease and not the lung disease (cardiac means, of the heart).
Corticosteroid	One of the hormones secreted by the adrenal glands. Given as tablet, injection or inhaler in asthma cases to reduce constriction of the bronchi.
Cromoglycate sodium	A drug, which if inhaled by an asthma patient, does not allow spasm of the bronchi even if he is exposed to an allergen.
Cyanosed	Having bluish tinge of the skin and mucous membranes because of lessened quantity of oxygen in the blood.
Dander	Tiny scales that fall from the animals, skin and the hair.

Elimination diet	Eliminating one or more substances from from the diet for at least three weeks, and then introducing the eliminated food in the fourth week, and observing whether initially the symptoms decreased or disappeared and later on increased or appeared.
Emphysema	A condition in which there is permanent overinflation of the lungs. This occurs after long-standing asthma, bronchitis and smoking.
Eosinophil cells	A type of white blood cell (leucocyte). It number is increased in the blood in allergic conditions.
Eustachian tubes	Tubes that connect the inner ear with the throat.
Expectorant	A substance which makes it easy for the phlegm to cough out.
Gamma-globulin	A particular fraction of globulin, which is a protein.
Histamine	A chemical substance which is released in the body or part of the body as a results of antigen-antibody reaction. It dilates the small blood vessels, capillaries, so that fluid from the blood pours into the tissues. In the skin, this fluid occurs as urticaria, in seasonal sneezing as running nose and in asthma as phlegm.
House dust	This is a mixture of many substances. It is what you collect after cleaning and dusting the house. It contains street dust, human and animal hair and dander, fibres from the linen and clothing, remnants of food and insects and another thing, lately discovered, a house-dust mite.

Hyposensitization	A processing of increasing resistance of the body to an allergen by means of small increasing injection of the allergens.
IgE	The word is abbreviation of immunoglobulin E. E is a particular fraction of the globulin found in cases of asthma and other allergies.
Mast cell	It is the cell in the tissues of the body on whose outer surface the IgE is fixed.
Mite	A small microscopic insect that can live on the human and animal hair and dander that has been shed. In the house, it is discovered in plenty in the mattresses and the house dust. This mite is considered to be the allergen in those who are sensitive to house-dust. Mite extract gives a more severe reaction in those who are allergic to house dust.
Mucous membrane	The covering membrane of the passages and cavities of the body, such as the respiratory tract.
Mucus	A slimy substance that comes with the running nose or phlegm.
Neti	A yogic procedure of cleaning the nose.
Paranasal sinuses	Sinuses (air-spaces) around the nose, in the face.
Peptic ulcer	Ulcer in the stomach.
Perennial	Which remains or occurs the year round.
Pulmonary (lung) function tests	The patient is asked to breathe or blow in different manners into a machine. Thereby inspiration volume of air and

	expiration volume of air etc., is measured and also how fast the air moves in the air-ways of the lungs. This test is useful in cases of asthma. A simplified test, Peak-Flow meter, can tell the patient how well his lungs are working daily or at any time of the day.
Reagin	A kind of antibody present in the skin. Biochemically, it is identified as IgE.
Serotonin	One of the many substances liberated in an antigen-antibody reaction. Its effect is not relieved by antihistamines.
Salbutamol	A beta-stimulator bronchodilator.
Spirometry	Blowing or breathing in a machine called spirometer, which measures lung volumes and the rate of flow of air in the bronchi
Spores	The 'seeds' of the fungus.
Status asthmaticus	A severe attack of asthma which has lasted more than 24 hours and has not been relieved in spite of giving the usual drugs.
Tuberculin syringe	This is a special syringe which can measure and show very small quantities of injections. It has a capacity of 1 ml and can measure as small a quantity as 0.01 ml.
Vastra-Dhauti	Vastra means cloth; dhauti cleaning. It means a yogic procedure for cleaning with a cloth.
Vial dust	A sealed small glass bottle.

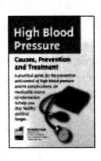

Dear Reader,

Welcome to the world of **Orient Paperbacks** — India's largest selling paperbacks in English. We hope you have enjoyed reading this book and would want to know more about **Orient Paperbacks**.

There are more than 700 **Orient Paperbacks** on a variety of subjects to entertain and inform you. The list of authors published in **Orient Paperbacks** includes, amongst others, distinguished and well-known names such as Dr. S. Radhakrishnan, R.K. Narayan, Raja Rao, John Buchanan, Khushwant Singh, Anita Desai, Greg Chappell, Dr. O.P. Jaggi, H.K. Bakhru, Norman Vincent Peale, Robert Schuller, Windy Dryden and Paul Hauck. **Orient Paperbacks** truly represent the best of Indian writing in English today.

We would be happy to keep you continuously informed of the new titles and programmes of **Orient Paperbacks** through our monthly newsletter, **Orient Literary Review**. Send in your name and full address to us today. We will send you **Orient Literary Review** completely free of cost.

Write for the complete catalogue.
Books available at all bookshops or by V.P.P.

Orient Paperbacks
5A/8, Ansari Road, New Delhi-110 002
www.orientpaperbacks.com